The **7** **BIGGEST MISTAKES**

made by

PROPERTY INVESTORS

and how to

AVOID THEM

A Platinum Partners Press Book

First published in Great Britain in 2009
by Platinum Partners Press

This book is not intended to provide personalised legal,
financial or investment advice. Readers should seek
professional advice with regard to such matters as interpretation
of the law, proper accounting procedures, financial planning
and tax before proceeding with any property investments. The
Authors and the Publisher specifically disclaim any liability, loss
or risk which is incurred as a consequence, directly or indirectly,
of the use and application of any contents of this work.

ISBN-13 978-0-9563646-0-9

Cover image © Platinum Partners Press, 2009
Cover design © Chris Goodier, cAPS lOCK iS oN, 2009

Copyright © 2009 by Steve Bolton and Nick Carlile

The right of Steve Bolton and Nick Carlile to be identified
as the authors of this work has been asserted by them in
accordance with the Copyright, Designs and
Patents Act, 1988.

All rights reserved. No part of this publication may be
reproduced, transmitted in any form or by any means, or stored
in a retrieval system without either the prior written permission
of the publisher, or in the case of reprographic reproduction a
licence issued in accordance with the terms and licences issued
by the CLA Ltd.

Praise for Steve Bolton, Nick Carlile and 'The 7 Biggest Mistakes Made by Property Investors and How to Avoid Them'

"Steve, Nick and the team at Platinum Property Partners are the leading edge investment experts and advisors in Europe today. Their meticulous attention to detail is obvious from the consistently high returns enjoyed by their Partners and investors. They are experienced in helping ambitious individuals achieve their financial goals with greater ease and assurance."
- Brian Tracy, best selling author and international speaker

"Over the last 10 years I've met many companies claiming to make people rich from property investment, but found few I felt I could trust and even fewer deals that were worth the money. Meeting Steve and Nick was a complete breath of fresh air. They clearly understand – and talk openly about – the pros and cons of property investment. They appreciate it's not for everyone and that 'no money down deals' and 'get rich quick schemes' don't work. Having spent quite some time with Nick and Steve over the last 12 months, I believe they really understand how to make money from property and, more importantly, how they can help other people make money. And what's really refreshing is the open and transparent environment in which they deliver this."
- Kate Faulkner, author, the Which? essential property guides; broadcast commentator; Managing Director, Designs on Property

"Steve Bolton and Nick Carlile are those rare kind of entrepreneurs who work in collaboration with everyone they meet, sharing the spoils of their extraordinary knowledge with those who also seek business success. They have built their property empires the hard way - through trial and error – and, put quite simply, Steve and Nick know what works. If you are considering any venture which relates to property I urge you to read this book first."
- Rachel Elnaugh, Entrepreneur, business author and ex-Dragons' Den panellist

"Platinum Property Partners are shining and (in my view) lone beacons of integrity, professionalism and true expertise in the

field of property investor education and property business start up and growth. I can highly recommend PPP, the Franchise systems and Steve Bolton personally as best-in-class providers."
- Jonathan Jay, Founder of SuccessTrack, presenter of TV's 'Get a New Life' and 'Now I'm The Boss', and best-selling author

"Steve Bolton literally transforms people's thinking and behaviour to help them create highly effective systems of ethically-based prosperity, regardless of their background and economic situation. The results are quite amazing. My friends who have employed his services are forever and positively changed!"
- Tim Redmond, President, Redmond Leadership Institute and author

"Nick Carlile impressed me on the very first occasion that we met and as I have got to know him well I have grown to appreciate the person and the businessman for his wisdom and integrity. Nick's quiet, unassuming style belies an inner strength and sense of purpose. His and Steve's extensive knowledge of the property world, and ability to discover and embrace new ideas, enables PPP to push out the boundaries and stay ahead of the field."
- Philip Easter, Former Finance Director, Norwich Union and Aviva PLC; PPP Franchise Partner

"Thanks to Steve, Nick and PPP I have built a substantial, income producing, multi-million pound property portfolio, and I am proud and very pleased to have Steve as a mentor. His passion, charisma, industry knowledge, and his desire to see others succeed is the reason I have chosen to work with him and Nick, and will continue to do so, on both a personal and business level."
- Caroline Marsh, C4 'Secret Millionaire' and PPP Franchise Partner

"Steve and Nick's knowledge, passion and commitment to successful property investment is legendary. Read this book and learn."
- David Oliver, Managing Director, Insight Marketing; Associate Director of The UK Marketing Guild

"I have been in business for over 26 years and have been extremely impressed by the size and expertise of the franchise business that Steve and Nick have established. They and their extremely

competent team at Platinum Property Partners provide a second to none service to their clients, and I feel sure even greater things lie ahead for Steve, Nick and anyone that chooses to fly in their slipstream."
- Chris Wilkins, Senior Partner, Wilkins Southworth Chartered Certified Accountants and Registered Auditors

"Steve and Nick are true professionals, and over the past few years I have seen the results of the way they have developed the skill sets of a wide range of individuals, helping them build successful property portfolios. Their shared enthusiasm to explore different commercial activities and strategies is matched only by the pleasure they get from seeing great success achieved by individuals they have mentored."
- Andrew Stanway, Consultant, Collier Financial Ltd

"This book is unquestionably one of the best preparation tools you could have if you're thinking of starting out in property investment, and an enjoyable and thought-provoking read for those of us already in the business. Steve and Nick's wealth of experience shines through, with some excellent business principles and robust methods for maximising profitability, and the altruistic approach they and their Partners take is an inspiration."
- Randeesh Sandhu, co-founder Urban Exposure Ltd; author, 'The Meaningful Life: How to Live The Life You Love and Love The Life You Live'.

"Steve Bolton belongs to that rare breed of property investment entrepreneurs who act with honesty and integrity at all times. He has experienced highs and lows in a multi-faceted business career and this experience has proved to be invaluable in helping him to source the right deals at the right time. There is no doubt that without Steve and Nick's energetic and sympathetic guidance, my progress in building an ever growing, cash positive property portfolio would have been far slower and riddled with mistakes."
- Michael Dixon, Property Investor and PPP Franchise Partner

"Steve epitomises the true professional with 'abundance mentality'. Whilst his entrepreneurial appetite seems to be insatiable, Steve's desire and ethic to "GIVE More" is a testimony and insight into his extremely generous and caring nature. His

continuous flow of innovative commercial activities and ventures stem from his incredible ability to unleash the full and latent potential in individuals and organisations."
- Barry Bailey, Managing Director, Mobile Team Challenge Ltd; former EMEA Marketing Director for 3M

"In today's uncertain world, business acumen and experience remain as important as ever, but without character and integrity they are worth very little. Steve combines them all. He reminds us that profit is not an end in its self, but rather enables entrepreneurs to accomplish their own personal goals. I hope that this book will help to develop many more truly successful investors."
- Lionel Stock, General Manager, Jonathan Faith Investments; formerly Financial Director, Faith Footwear Ltd.

"I have known Steve and Nick for two years and have come to respect not only their knowledge of property investment but also their ethical, no-nonsense approach to business and their aim to ensure that all parties benefit from any deal. This book is a must both for old hands and novices to property investing alike."
- Mike Withey, Founder, The London Property Network

"In my 25+ years experience in the Real Estate business I have seen it all. There are pure nuggets of gold in what Steve and Nick have to say. Their knowledge as real estate investors, the level of detail they share and the stress tests they apply to new ideas and strategies are the marks of true professionals."
- John B. Corey Jr., Managing Director, Chelsea Private Equity

"Steve Bolton and Nick Carlile definitely know their onions when it comes to all aspects of property investment. They are happy to share their knowledge and have a knack of conveying it in a delightfully calm, succinct manner. Behind those rye smiles are very sharp minds, which place great value on integrity, both in business and personal relationships."
- Tom Overton, PPP Investment Partner

"Steve is one of the most intuitive and naturally gifted businesspeople I have come across in 15 years of working in UK and international property investment. His ability to identify

opportunities and develop strategies which maximise short, medium and long-term profitability, combined with his love of and skill in helping others succeed, makes him truly exceptional. The rapid growth and success of the PPP franchise is testament to his energy, focus and desire to build partnerships that create and share wealth. Steve is not only a trusted business partner but also an inspiring and valued friend."
- Richard Davies, Founding Partner, Platinum Partners Group; Founder and former Investment Director, Visium Group; author, 'Property Developer Secrets'

"I am really glad our path led us to Nick and Steve. The property business has gained a bit of a bad name over the years and it was enormously refreshing to find a hugely successful business dealing in property, run by individuals with high values and integrity. Steve and Nick walk the talk and really want to make the world a better place. They have very sharp business minds, and have created so much already, but are always looking forward."
- Philip Clemo, Composer and Property Investor

"In 2007 we were almost wiped out, having made a monumental mistake by investing in the wrong property. Though they didn't know us personally at the time, only our predicament, Steve and Nick helped us every step of the way to come out of the mess with minimal financial impact and put us on the path to a wonderfully successful property investing business that has blessed us and enables us to be a blessing."
- Isaac Samuel, Distinguished Member of Technical Staff, Alcatel-Lucent

"I am a professional private psychiatrist and own about £10m of property. Which has taken most time? The profession. Which has made most money? The property. I have known Steve and Nick for a few years and one mistake that you can't make is listening to them. I have no doubt that I would have tripped up less, and made more, if I had met them a long time ago."
- Dr. Robin Lawrence, Psychiatrist and PPP Franchise Partner

"We first met Steve about a year ago and quickly realized that his knowledge and expertise in the property industry is second to none. He has unconditionally helped us with his time and expertise to move forward in some of our property ventures. His positive energy, knowledge and willingness to help sets a

fantastic example to all his Franchise Partners and the team around him."
- Juswant and Sylvia Rai, Founders and Hosts of the Berkshire Property Meet

"We are continually impressed with Steve and Nick's drive, zest and enthusiasm when working with their business partners in overcoming and resolving the issues that the current economic climate has presented. Their knowledge of the property industry is second to none and this is reflected in the creative solutions that are always forthcoming. And despite the extremely busy demands of their lives, they always have time for us and are really fun, supportive and inspiring guys!"
- Mike and Lucy Regan, PPP Franchise Partners

"During the 25 years I have been involved in property, I have had the pleasure - or otherwise - of meeting different characters within the industry and confess to rarely having a good word for any of them! Steve and Nick not only live by the values they teach, but do it with such humility. Today, more than ever, our time is precious, but time spent with and learning from Steve and Nick will never be time wasted."
- Brian Stevenson, Property Developer

"Steve has been an inspiring speaker at our European Business Achievers Conference and I have personally recommended him as a mentor to a number of prospective investors throughout the UK. He is entrepreneurial but with an altruistic value system and a genuine desire to help others succeed in life. He is a pioneer, a visionary and able to replicate his methodologies and success in the property industry so as to benefit others."
- Keith Chapman-Burnett, Pastor, House of Destiny

"Steve could have applied his natural entrepreneurial skills to any field of endeavour, but the property market, particularly of late, has allowed him to use his flare for adaptability, ingenuity and shear dogged perseverance to maximum effect. Steve is a charismatic and inspiring mentor and role model, who has an uncanny knack for seeing and nurturing the best in people. I describe him as someone who 'you may not know for sure exactly where they're headed, but you sure as heck want in on the ride, so grab those shirt tails and hang on!' I'm hanging on and loving the ride!"
- Judy Mizen, PPP Franchise Partner and former Physiotherapist

"The entrepreneur is our visionary,
the creator in each of us."
- Michael Gerber

The 7 BIGGEST MISTAKES

made by

PROPERTY INVESTORS

and how to

AVOID THEM

Steve Bolton

Nick Carlile

Platinum Partners Press, 2009

BE MORE – DO MORE – HAVE MORE – GIVE MORE ®

Contents

This book is dedicated to:

*Lucy, Nathan, Charlie, Ella, Jude,
Ronnie, Lydie and Michelle Bolton,
the true sources of my inspiration
and motivation.*

*A huge thanks also to
Sarah Walker, without whom this book
would not have been possible.*

Steve

*For Emma and Thomas,
who keep me focused on the
truly important things that life
has to offer.*

Nick

About the Authors

Steve Bolton

Entrepreneurial flair surfaced early in Steve. At the age of 8 he was following stocks and shares and by 11 he was gambling pocket money on horses! But like many other highly successful entrepreneurs, the traditional education system failed him and he left school at 16 with no qualifications. By 30 he had made his first million.

Steve is now one of the UK's most well-respected and successful property investors and business entrepreneurs and is highly regarded as an inspirational keynote speaker. He currently owns five very profitable businesses, including a substantial, multi-million pound, income-producing UK portfolio, and has a lead interest in international property projects worth over £50 million.

So how did he get from being an unqualified teen to his first million? Determination to succeed, a love of the outdoors and a natural flair for teaching others led Steve to an apprenticeship working in outdoor pursuits, where he started to realise his own potential. He moved on a few years later and set up his first business, Ropes Course Developments, which built all the high and low adventure ropes courses for Center Parcs, First Choice Holidays and the RAF in Europe, as well as courses in 12 other countries. Once that was established, he started another business providing management consultancy and development training, servicing a number of well-known blue chip and other high-profile clients including the British Lions, Microsoft and KPMG. Steve had a beautiful house on the south coast, a great social life and two successful businesses, but then, as with most eventually successful entrepreneurial journeys, he hit a major bump in the road.

In the economic fallout that followed the terrorist attacks in America on 11th September 2001, Steve's businesses were all but wiped out, and he was forced to sell his own home to avoid going bankrupt. He credits that period as being "the best worst experience of my life". In being taken back to virtually nothing, he was shown the power of owning underlying assets. If he had owned his business premises which, over a 7 year period, in a fast-rising property market, would have translated into a substantial asset base, he probably could have ridden out the storm, but his company only rented the buildings. Steve learnt from this fundamental mistake and made sure he rebuilt his fortune on the solid foundation of property. He now helps others ensure they do the same.

Steve has appeared on television - on Sky's 'Property Pensions', 'Head to Head' and 'Property Kings' - and featured in the national press, including the Financial Times and the Institute of Directors Magazine. He regularly contributes to other property, franchise and business start up publications, giving expert opinion and comment and personal interviews.

Away from his business commitments, Steve is a keen sportsman: he has played tennis at club level and has also been a semi-professional footballer. He enjoys fishing and working on his boat in Poole Harbour, flying helicopters, and always strives to be a better parent and husband. Thanks to the financial freedom he has achieved, he has chosen to take three months off every year since 2004 to spend quality time with his wife and family, travelling the world and helping them to get a varied and balanced education. Steve is also the lead patron of Peace One Day - www.peaceoneday.org - which is dedicated to achieving global ceasefire and non-violence for one day every year, on September 21st, and is ratified by the U.N. He is actively involved in recruiting new patrons and fundraising and sits on the executive board of Patrons.

Steve lives in Bournemouth, on the south coast, with his wife, Lucy, four children – Nathan, Charlie, Ella and Jude - and their dog, Jazzie. Most weeks he also spends time in London, meeting with potential and existing Platinum Partners.

Nick Carlile

A qualified Quantity Surveyor, Nick has worked in the property construction and investment industry since the age of 16. He has purchased and renovated a variety of properties in and around South Yorkshire, and presently has a multi-million pound property portfolio in the UK, as well as a number of investments in Eastern Europe. From building his own home in Barnsley to managing large-scale international development projects worth hundreds of millions, Nick has a wealth of experience in the field and has written - and continues to deliver – one of the UK's leading courses in self build and development.

Nick's route to success was a little more traditional than Steve's, in that he enjoyed school and did very well academically. After his GCSEs he was given the opportunity to work as a surveyor's apprentice, and leapt at the chance

- it was a simple choice between staying on to do A' levels and earning nothing, earning £29.50 a week under the Government's Youth Training Scheme, or taking home £40.00 a week as a surveyor's apprentice!

From 1991 to 2005, Nick worked for various construction and development companies in Yorkshire, initially as a Quantity Surveyor and latterly as a Project Manager. He was responsible for the legal, financial and overall project management of a number of developments in Sheffield, including: over 400 apartments and retail units in the centre – still the largest of its kind in the city; a £6m student accommodation block, which was completed within 9 months; the £20m conversion of Victorian hospital buildings to form luxury dwellings on the outskirts, and the construction of 133 other dwellings in the city with a GDV of £13m.

He worked on the early stages of the scheme to regenerate the entire estate of Norfolk Park, including the overall Masterplan, and managed a nationwide partnership scheme for the delivery of nursing homes for one of the UK's leading care providers. Identifying and managing the risk associated with development projects – carrying out a very high level of due diligence and ensuring the legal side is watertight and all parties are treated fairly - is a key skill of Nick's and one of the reasons why people are confident in doing business with him.

Nick bought his first house when he was 19 and continued to buy property over the following 10 years, but it wasn't until 2004 that he decided to move in to property investing as a full time career.

Says Nick, "For me property is the best investment I can

make. It's something I understand, it's tangible and unlike shares, which can be wiped out overnight, property always retains some value. There are thousands of micro-markets in the UK and successful property investing is about understanding these micro markets in the short and long term."

Nick lives in Bournemouth with his wife, Emma, and young son, Thomas. He divides his time between the South coast, Yorkshire and London, joining Steve in meeting with current and prospective Platinum business partners. Nick is committed to giving back to charitable causes: as well as entering the Great North Run every year, he's also jumped out of a plane, taken part in the '3 Peaks Challenge' and, alongside Steve, is an active patron of Peace One Day.

The Platinum Partners Group of Companies

Both Steve and Nick excel in and are passionate about mentoring other investors, business owners and entrepreneurs, to enable them to achieve financial freedom and a better quality of life. The vehicle for achieving that is the Platinum Partners Group of companies, which Steve and Nick have founded, together with a third business partner, Richard Davies. Platinum Property Partners is the lead company in the Group and is the world's first buy to let property investing franchise. It is one of the fastest growing start up franchises in the UK and considered a 'best in class' business opportunity. The June 2009 NatWest/bfa franchise survey reported that most franchisees' businesses break even by the end of the second year of trading; if Franchise Partners follow the PPP cash-positive investment model, they see profit on turnover from the start. Through a combination of one to one intensive initial mentoring and excellent ongoing business and personal support and training, Franchise Partners are building multi-million pound property portfolios which are achieving market-leading returns.

For those who have neither the time nor desire to be active property investors but who still want to benefit from the returns property can offer, and create or diversify an investment portfolio, there is a Passive Investment Partnership. Platinum Portfolio Builder allows passive investors to have a UK portfolio built and managed on their behalf, and the Passive Loans programme provides guaranteed monthly returns on capital. The Group also comprises: Platinum Investment Partners, which sources and manages low risk, high return international projects for investors; Platinum Business Partners, which helps turn around and grow specially selected businesses; and the Platinum Partners Foundation, the charitable arm of the company.

The mission of the Platinum Partners Group is to inspire, mentor and support others to BE more, DO more, HAVE more and GIVE more in life, and Steve and Nick are determined that everyone they and their team work with should strive to make a difference. 10% of the Group's profits go to charitable causes - including orphanages in India and Uganda, and community projects in Toxteth - and the aim in this non-profit work is to achieve effective and sustainable giving, enabling projects to become self-sufficient over time. All the Founders and some of their Platinum Partners are Patrons of Peace One Day.

Editor's Note

This book is written from Steve Bolton's perspective for the purposes of fluidity and clarity, although it has been co-authored by Nick Carlile and the content is drawn from both entrepreneurs' experiences in property and business. The business models outlined, and opinions and advice given, are practiced and shared by Steve and Nick, and their Platinum Partners.

Foreword

by Sarah Walker,
Presenter of BBC1's 'To Buy Or Not To Buy',
freelance property writer and home image consultant,
and Platinum Property Partners Franchise Partner.

When I first got to know Steve, around five years ago, he was full of excitement about a new property investor education programme he had designed and asked if I would help him and his team deliver some introductory seminars to various groups around the country. Everyone already involved was so energetic, professional and genuinely inspiring that I had no hesitation in joining them.

Over the course of the next 12 months it became apparent that what people were crying out for was not only information and training specifically tailored to their individual requirements, but ongoing support and continual access to a team they could rely on to give professional advice, ensuring they stayed ahead of the property investment field. Steve found in Nick someone who shared his enthusiasm and whose background and experience perfectly complemented his own. Together, they dedicated themselves to refining and delivering a systemised approach to helping others replicate the success they had achieved with their own property portfolios, and built up a 'power team' of over 33 'best in class' property, legal and financial advisors. The combination of the system and the team ultimately became the Platinum Property Partners franchise business.

In order to help explain to aspiring investors and potential Franchise Partners the value of mentoring and following a tried and tested system versus going it alone, Steve and Nick put together a presentation highlighting the potential pitfalls in property investing and showing how they could be avoided. That presentation, which has proved hugely popular in countless talks and keynote speeches to property investors and entrepreneurs around the UK, provided the basis for this book.

I've worked in the property field for the last ten years – initially as an estate agent in Berkshire and Surrey, then as a property programme presenter for BBC1, and latterly as a speaker and freelance property writer – and I consider myself to be pretty well informed about the market. I've been around a lot of property seminars, shows and events, and seen all the big players in the UK 'property investment education' field. For me, PPP, led by Steve and Nick, stands head and shoulders above the competition in terms of ethical business practice, robust business models, expertise, integrity, and downright common sense.

The fact that the business has continued to thrive, and its Partners continued to make profits in 2007, 2008 and 2009, during one of the worst financial crises in the last 100 years, is real evidence of the tried, tested and proven nature of PPP's strategies.

Much of the advice in this book – drawn from years of refining highly profitable property investment strategies and Steve's vast experience in start-up ventures – can also be applied outside the property sphere and will undoubtedly improve the way you approach any business, as well as your own personal life.

I've been mentored personally by Steve, worked closely with him and Nick for the past 3 years, and as a PPP Franchise Partner I'm currently building a cash-positive portfolio in Poole, Dorset, using PPP's franchise systems. I have also invested passively with PPP into a project in Romania and entered into a guaranteed and secure passive loan arrangement, which provides market-beating monthly interest returns.

If you're a novice investor, this book will prove an invaluable tool in preparing to fast-track your success, and if you're a seasoned professional, it should provide an injection of fresh ideas and motivation, backed by tried, tested and proven strategies for making substantial profits in any market. In either case, it will be a valuable investment of your time, and I hope you'll enjoy it as much as I have!

*"There are three constants in life...
change, choice and principles."*
Stephen R. Covey

Chapter 1
Introduction

There are lots of books already out there, written by icons of the business and property world, that give fantastic advice, much of which can be life-changing for those who read them, and I include myself in that category. I'm not trying to compete with the greats here, but from what I've heard from people I speak to every day, there's clearly a need for something that communicates the core principles of property investing as a business, particularly for the UK market, because there are still too many investors out there making fundamental mistakes.

It frustrates me talking to people who have started investing in property and made some really basic errors that have cost them a huge amount of time and money – bad decisions they can't reverse. Sometimes these are people who've bought and sold a few of their own homes and think that's more or less all there is to property investing, so they've leapt in blindly. Other times I meet people who have been investing for a number of years and consider themselves experienced, but have actually made money more though luck and a rising market, rather than because of any particular strategy or business plan, so when the going gets tough, they flounder.

Increasingly I'm coming across investors with portfolios that used to break even, or perhaps needed just a slight monthly subsidy, but since the credit crunch hit, a lot of their properties are now significantly cash-negative and they can't re-finance. As at mid-2009, many are only surviving due to the record-breaking low interest rates, which cannot and will not go on for ever. That leaves them stuck with a portfolio that's not doing what they thought it would, and them, personally, on shaky financial ground, and it's an awful situation for anyone to find themselves in.

I understand, because I've been in the position where overlooking some fundamental business principles left me on the verge of bankruptcy, and one of the main reasons for writing this book is to help other people avoid getting into that kind of situation. Property is a superb wealth-creation vehicle, and if you can just get a heads-up on how to overcome some of the challenges that trip so many people, you're giving yourself a much better chance of success. Whether you already have a portfolio and need to realign your goals, or are experienced in some other field and looking to start investing in property, this book will highlight some of the main mistakes that investors make, and give you solutions you can apply not only to your property business, but to your life and, indeed, business as a whole.

BE MORE – DO MORE – HAVE MORE – GIVE MORE ®

My personal mission, and the mission of our company, is very much based around inspiring, mentoring and supporting people to be more, do more, have more and give more. A lot of the time people just focus on the 'have more': "I want a new car, I want a new house, etc...". What is less commonly understood is the fact that anybody who creates sustainable wealth, financial freedom and time freedom is not benefiting completely from what they *do*, but from who and what they *are*. People who have all-round success in lots of areas in their life tend to be fundamentally positive, optimistic, giving, dedicated people. They achieve success in probably the broadest sense of the word, and it's driven by the person that they are. I define success holistically: in simple terms, that means being happy, fulfilled, healthy, wealthy, and contributing to others every day in a positive and meaningful way.

Who you are encompasses a huge variety of factors, but in terms of building a property business it's probably most importantly about self-confidence, time and money management and communication skills. Property is a people business, first and foremost. You need to have excellent negotiation skills, people have to like and want to work with you, and you must always do business with integrity. In order to be as successful as you can, you need to understand fundamentals about how money works as well as apply principles of success that relate to every business. The message I'm trying to get across is that if people start with DO more and HAVE more, they're actually missing out on the key to it all - the BE element. Simply put, your personal and professional development is the most important ingredient for your future success. As the saying goes, "The more you learn, the more you earn."

That success leads on to being able to GIVE more, and not simply in terms of money. As your business grows, your passive income will bring you increasing time freedom, and the opportunity to give back by sharing your knowledge, experience, money, time and skills with others.

Why property is the right vehicle

In 2001 I was in America, listening to two very successful real estate investors called Robert G. Allen and Glen Purdy, and they made a statement that had a really big impact on me. They said,

"90% of the world's wealth is either made from, or held in property."

I don't know where they got that figure from, and haven't been able to find out since, but if you look at the Times Rich List and other sources that compile records of the very wealthy, you'll see that a huge number list property as having contributed directly to their fortune. The largest single category on the Rich List is Property and Construction. Even where property is not directly listed, many of those people have invested a large portion of their money in commercial and residential property around the world.

---

192 of the top 500 on the Times Rich List 2008 (38.4%) listed property as having directly contributed to their current wealth. The figure rises to 42% when you look at the top 100.

It's also very obvious to everyone who's owned property for any period of time that medium to long term it goes up in value, and the more you have, the more your fortune in equity increases.

That makes it very simple for me: if you're going to choose a field on which to play your game of business and making money, then surely it makes sense to pick one that is proven to have created such a huge amount of wealth. History is certainly no guarantee of the future, but just look at where the very wealthy are continuing to hedge their bets for long-term security.

Capital appreciation is a given over time, but it's only one of a whole host of fundamental and robust reasons why it can be the perfect key to financial freedom - and this book will explain a number of others.

Surprisingly few people view property as a business that can provide you with a passive monthly income that exceeds your monthly outgoings, and I'll talk about this cashflow-positive investing model in greater detail later on. Suffice to say, property is, for me, the Holy Grail: it gives you profitable and sustainable business growth, underpinned by an ever-increasing asset base.

Why should you trust what I say?

The short answer is: you shouldn't! What I really mean by that is you should always have a healthy amount of scepticism when people are giving you advice and question whether they're the best person to be listening to. Everyone has an opinion about property, and everyone knows there's nobody quicker to advise you than 'the man in the pub' and the more vocal members of your family and friends! So ask yourself what this person has done themselves, whether you admire their achievements, and whether those are the same things you want to achieve.

If you're looking to learn about property investing from somebody, what kind of person would you want to learn from? You can't beat a proven track record, so find someone who's done what you want to do and make sure they've had the hard knocks and really overcome adversity in a diverse range of situations. It's also vital you like and trust them, because that personal relationship – being able to trust someone and also enjoy their company – is so important when you're taking big steps and making probably some of the biggest investments of your life.

And don't be dazzled by paper qualifications, I'm talking about real, on-the-ground experience that can't be studied at school or university. I don't have a single academic qualification. When I was at school I had a pretty good chance of passing two O' Levels: French, because my mother is French, and Maths, because I happened to be good with figures.

In the French exam I finished the paper in about half an hour then did what I thought was the decent thing (!) and passed it round my friends to help them out. A little unfairly, I thought, I was disqualified; needless to say, my mother wasn't happy!

The Maths paper turned out to be a bit harder than I expected and there was one question I just couldn't get. I had the brainbox of the class sitting in front of me, so I tried to get his attention to ask him to help me with the answer, but he kept ignoring me. In the end I pulled out my compass to give him a little prod, but it slipped and went in a bit harder than I meant it to. The result: a squeal from him, blood all over the back of his shirt and an automatic fail for me!

Has my lack of qualifications hindered my success? It's hard to say for sure, but I don't think so. By 18 I had a job I loved, at 24 I was headhunted to set up an outdoor pursuits centre and by 26 I had found a partner and we were launching a business that extended its operations worldwide. It wasn't easy, but because I had to rely purely on common sense, logic, trial and error and hard work, it made me the businessman I am today. My years of experience in business start up, management training and development and property investing stand alone as my qualifications, and I truly don't think academic success would have made me any better in business, or more successful or happy, personally or professionally.

"Success leaves clues."
- Tony Robbins

If you want to fast-track your own success, it's quite simple: make sure you learn from experts who have achieved what you want to achieve, in a way that you would be happy to replicate.

I've had over twelve business and ten business partners since 1994, and I've made multi-million pound businesses several times over. Some of those I've kept, some I've sold for profit, but I've also had to put a company into voluntary liquidation and come close to personal bankruptcy. I chose to rebuild my fortune on the solid foundation of a highly cash-positive property portfolio, which gives me the freedom to choose how, when and with whom I spend my time. That's also something I have been privileged to be able to show others how to do.

I've worked with private investors and raised multi-million pounds worth of funding. I've run out of investment capital in my property investing career and solved that problem, working out how to leverage other people's time and money to keep my portfolio expanding. I've had the privilege of having some very capable business partners who are phenomenal experts and specialists in their own field, and I've spent over a hundred thousand pounds of my own money in the last 10 years travelling the world to learn from multi-millionaires and billionaires, in property and business.

Both I and my business partners are genuinely passionate about helping other people be more, do more, have more, and give more, and create financial freedom in their lives. If this is a message that resonates with you, I sincerely hope this book will act as a catalyst for positive and lasting change in your life. I also hope one day to be able to meet you personally.

Fundamental Principles
in Property Investing

- Strive to BE more, DO more, HAVE more and GIVE more in your life.
- Remember that property is, first and foremost, a people business.
- Have an abundance mentality – help others get what they want, and you'll find they'll help you in return.
- 90% of the world's wealth is either made from, or held in property, so add this income/asset stream to your life.
- Property investment, executed properly, should give you profitable and sustainable business growth, with an appreciating asset base.
- Don't forget: Cashflow is King!

Chapter 2

Starting Out in Property Investment

Presumably you've picked up this book because you've decided property is what you want to focus on, and that's great, but you need to make sure you're not only aware of what you're getting into, but that you're fully equipped to succeed. Property is not for everyone, for many different reasons, and too many people think that as long as they have a positive attitude and determination, that's enough to see them through. While those are certainly essential attributes, there are a lot of other variables to consider, and you need to have a thorough reality check before setting off on this journey.

Before you start...

It may sound obvious, but the first thing you need to do is decide exactly *why* you want to get into property investing. Too many people dive into it because they know property makes sense as an investment, but they don't spend enough time thinking about what they actually want to get out of it and they don't have clear enough timescales. When I hear people complaining that an investment hasn't done for them what they had thought it would, although sometimes that's been the result of not doing enough due diligence, it's often fundamentally because their expectations were either misaligned, unrealistic or, in most cases, not even defined properly.

You need to spend some time thinking about your

objectives, goals and desires. When you're going on any kind of journey - which this is: starting a new business or accelerating a business you've already got – you need to work out what your destination is, have some clear written objectives, and apply a time frame to them. These objectives may change as you move forward, and you need to review them regularly, but you should certainly be able to be specific about the next twelve months and have some idea about where you want to be in five and ten years' time. And be realistic – you're not going to become a multi-millionaire property investor in just a few months, from a standing start. Property isn't a 'get rich quick' business, it's a 'get *very* rich, over time' business and you need to plan for the medium to long term if you're serious about creating something meaningful, with sustainability and longevity.

The most extreme example I can give of unrealistic goals and expectations is a young lady I spoke to several years ago. She had paid £5,000 to attend a weekend property training seminar organised by a company that promised the earth but delivered very little. Having found that the theoretical training didn't work in the real world, she contacted Platinum Property Partners to find out if we would send one of our mentors to work with her in the field and show her how professional investors operate. One of our investment directors asked what capital she had to invest and what her goals were and she said, "I want to own a £10 million portfolio in 12 months and I have £10,000 of starting capital." Now, we like to encourage people to push the boundaries of what is possible, but in this case the young lady needed to be given some direct feedback that what she was aiming for was totally unrealistic.

11

Her response was that she'd been told it was possible when she booked to go on the course. We asked whether that was before or after she'd made the £5,000 payment and, not surprisingly, she told us it was before. Our final piece of advice to her was to go back to the company and either ask for her money back or insist that they deliver on the promise to give her value, but we doubt she ever got any kind of return for her investment. Caveat Emptor - buyer beware!!

If you're sceptical about the usefulness or effectiveness of writing down your plans, this illustration might make a difference:

In 1979, Harvard Business School conducted a survey of students on its MBA programme, asking how many of them had clear, written goals for their future and plans for how they would achieve them. Only 3% had actually written them down, a further 13% had unwritten goals, and the remaining 84% didn't have any specific goals at all. Ten years later, in 1989, the same group was interviewed again. Those with unwritten goals were each earning around twice as much as those without any goals at all, and the 3% who had written their goals and plans down were found to be earning, on average, ten times as much as the other 97% put together *(from 'What they don't teach you at Harvard Business School' by Mark McCormack).*

It's also proven over time that the further ahead you can project, the more accurate your plans will turn out to be, so although you might find detailing five and ten year goals much harder than those for the next twelve months, taking the time to do it will pay dividends.

I was very fortunate, in the mid-1990s, to work with

Adrian Moorhouse, the British Olympic gold medal-winning swimmer. Adrian had retired from swimming and had started a management consultancy called Lane4, which he still has today. I was mentoring Adrian in the world of management development at the time and we were running outdoor management programmes together for the accountancy firm KPMG.

One evening I asked Adrian what he believed were the most important things that had led to his Olympic gold medal achievement. On top of the usual stuff you would expect to hear - extreme dedication, parental support, natural ability, etc - he also had 'visualisation' in his top five, and I was surprised.

He went on to tell me that he had swum the Olympic race in his head literally thousands of times before. He added that the way in which he won it was exactly how he had visualised it and he believed it was a critical success factor, not just in sport but in business as well. Mohamed Ali, the legendary boxer, used to call visualisation 'future history'. Ali was also an avid goal setter and visualiser. When he was quizzed by reporters after a rare defeat in the boxing ring, Ali stated that the reason for losing was because the other boxer's 'future history' was stronger than his.

Personally, I find making vision boards works best for focusing on my goals. I put images of the things I'm aiming for, or images that represent my goals, together on a sheet of paper and stick it somewhere I'll keep looking at it – above my cross-trainer and in my bathroom work best for me. If you're a parent, you can also have fun with your children; here's a vision board my son, Charlie, made when he was five:

Note the largest image – of a particularly attractive female in her underwear – hardly appropriate for a five-year old! But hear me out... Charlie was absolutely insistent it was included on his board, and when I asked why, he said that she was the kind of woman he'd like to marry when he was older. Put like that, I thought, "Who am I to deny my son his future wife?!" Lucy (my wife) wasn't very happy when she saw it, but 5-year olds can be very persuasive when they want something badly enough... and little Charlie got his way!

Once you have an idea of where you want to be and when, really think about what you're going to need, financially, in order to achieve those goals and live that life, because the 'how much' and 'when' will dictate the choices you make with your property investment portfolio. So are you focused mainly on some kind of pension provision for your later years; are you looking for an income that will allow you to give up your 'day job' and choose what work you take; do you simply want to grow your capital as quickly and securely as possible; are you already wealthy and want to grow your business to leave as a legacy; is your current business or portfolio no longer working for you…or is it a combination of some or all of these?

Perhaps it's simply about managing the wealth that you've already created. My business partners and I specialise in working with a lot of other high net worth individuals who have significant amounts of funds to invest and just want to turn that into more money, in order to create more freedom, security and choice in their lives. The people we choose to do business with are not only interested in amassing their own fortune, but have a philanthropic interest in helping others and sharing their wealth, both in terms of money and time. I believe that attitude and those values are fundamental to a successful business and to attaining long-lasting financial freedom.

Can you do what you want to do?

It's important that you're under no illusions about the amount of time you'll need to dedicate to achieving your goals, so look at how much you have available and are willing to commit. The average person in this country spends 20 hours a week watching television, but I don't know any entrepreneur or successful property investor that spends anywhere near that amount of time on their sofa.

What time you're willing to commit will drive whether you're an active or passive investor, because with just a couple of hours a week there's no way you can be an active investor and build a property business yourself, hands-on. My basic rule of thumb is if you can't or aren't willing to commit at least 10 hours a week to property investing, then you would be better suited as a passive investor. Put your money into investments that will still deliver a good return on your capital, but require none, or very little of your time. Bear in mind that the more active you are, the better your returns tend to be (as long as you make good decisions), especially in the UK market.

And make sure you place a value on your time – something that most people forget to do. It drives me crazy on TV shows like 'Property Ladder' when Sarah Beeny does the financial summary at the end. She covers the costs buts misses out two critical factors:

1. The opportunity/interest cost of the money used for deposit, refurbishment and fees.
2. The time invested by the so-called 'investors' doing the work.

Firstly, if someone invests, say, £50,000 into a project, there is a cost related to that money. If it is being borrowed from equity then there is interest incurred on the funds, e.g. £50,000 borrowed for 12 months at 5% interest costs

£2,500. If the money is coming from savings then there is an opportunity cost, which, depending on how else you would have invested the cash, would be at least 2%, from a bank savings account. Professional investors always factor this into their calculations.

Secondly, there is never any allowance for the investors' time. When Sarah Beeny tells them they've made a £20,000 profit on the project over a 12 month period, she makes no allowance for their time. £20k on a 12 month project is a loss-making venture in my eyes and it should be in yours also. If you are investing your time and money into your property business make sure you pay yourself a rate that makes sense. If you can't make a profit after this then seriously consider if you wouldn't be better suited to being a passive investor.

Next, how much money have you got? If you have less than £100k of capital available to invest, either in equity or liquid funds, then property is a pretty tough business to start in. My guidance to anyone in that situation would be to start with another job or business opportunity that requires a much lower cash input to begin with - perhaps another franchise or internet marketing business - and use that to build up your capital. You *can* make investments in property with £100k or less, but you won't build a meaningful business, in my opinion.

This is the main reason our business, Platinum Property Partners, doesn't accept new Franchise or Investment Partners unless they have £100,000 or more available funds to invest. A key principle in what we teach investors is recycling your capital so that you get the best return on investment, but because of various time and mortgage market constrictions - particularly as things are in the 2009 market - it's sometimes necessary to leave money in an investment for 6 months or more before you can legally recycle it. In order to be able to keep building your property business and taking advantage of opportunities that will give good cashflow and be solid medium and long-term investments, you do need a decent amount of operating capital.

While it's possible for professional investors to buy property using very little of their own money, that's certainly not something you should be considering if you're just starting out. I and my business and Franchise Partners have done numerous deals of this kind in our property investment careers, but that's with many years' experience, a strong team of legal and financial experts around us and a proven track record, plus other streams of income and capital reserves. It's so hard to get everything right in the beginning and property is very high-risk if you're putting all your eggs into the one basket in a business that's new to you. And whatever you do, don't believe the 'No Money Down Property Millionaire' hype, because that's all it is, hype. I strongly disagree with the 'get rich quick' merchants in the property game, who profit from selling false hope to aspiring investors who have little or no cash.

The more money you've got, the easier it is to invest in property, particularly in times of major market correction and threatening economic recession, as is the situation while I'm writing this. There are some great opportunities for acquiring properties at well below what their value would be in a healthy market - properties that will provide good cashflow today - but when lenders are highly risk-averse and the best opportunities often require some refurbishment, investors have to accept they'll need to tie up a fairly substantial amount of capital in the short to medium term. As a result, if you've got less than £100k you're not going to be able to create anything too meaningful in a short period of time, and if you're serious about using property investment to provide a route to financial freedom, it's not a one or two property business.

As an aside to building a substantial property business, I would encourage any of you, when buying your own home, to try to choose something that you can still retain ownership of when you move on. I'm not a fan of selling property if you can help it, so go for a property that could generate enough rent to cover the mortgage, ideally much more. That means when you come to move up or down the ladder you get a greater benefit from your investment than simply the capital appreciation accrued while you have lived there. You may be able to remortgage it as a buy-to-let, pull out most of the capital to put down as a deposit on your next purchase, and be left with a property that will pay for itself and hopefully bring you some extra income every month. Then you can continue to benefit from more capital appreciation in the medium to long term, on multiple properties. I often think that if my parents had done this just once, all those years ago, their retirement would have been so very different.

So that's the time and money questions covered; now you need to think about risk and attitude, because those criteria are just as important. Your personality type is one of the key factors which will contribute to either your success or failure in the property business. People who are very pessimistic, very analytical and don't necessarily like dealing with people will quickly find that property is not for them - or rather, they're not right for property - because, as we'll look at later, property is very much a people business. Having an optimistic, solution-oriented attitude is critical to your success because you'll find there will always be obstacles in your way as you build your portfolio. It might be running short of capital, changes to legislation, or simply tenant and property management issues. You need to be able to focus on the bigger picture and find your way through the problems you'll face.

This runs alongside having the 'right' attitude to risk and debt. You need to really think how you feel about getting yourself into hundreds of thousands or millions of pounds worth of debt, because by the time you've got 4 or 5 properties, it's highly likely that's what your mortgage borrowing will have hit. If that thought terrifies you, and you're not comfortable with the idea of having high loan-to-value borrowing on a property, then I'd suggest you keep reading. This book will help clarify just what property investing is all about and explain the value of debt and how, used correctly, it can be your friend. There is a big difference between 'good debt' and 'bad debt', which we'll clarify further in Chapter 7.

Without the right attitude you will miss opportunities, slow down your progress and may well stall before you've started. I've seen too many people hanging in limbo, permanently on the brink of 'doing something' – either what I call the 'shelf-help' (rather than self-help!) brigade, or 'course-junkies', who spend money going on lots of courses but never get round to applying what they learn.

Towards the end of the book we'll look at 'analysis paralysis' and how you can avoid that trap. For now, focus on thinking positively about what you can achieve, because great success is all about taking calculated risks. By that, I mean looking at the potential risks associated with an investment and making sure you understand them. Then you need to do sufficient due diligence so that those risks are either greatly reduced or eliminated. You must also be comfortable that the reward justifies the risk.

> *"If you don't risk anything,*
> *you risk even more."*
> **- Erica Jong**

Personal qualities of a successful investor:

- An optimist with an all-round positive attitude
- Solution-focused
- Action-oriented
- Excellent inter-personal skills
- Willingness to take a calculated risk
- An open mind
- Willingness to keep learning
- Little or no fear of failure and the ability to see it as feedback
- Thoughtfulness, generosity of spirit and selflessness
- Persistence
- Good/great money management skills
- Financially astute
- A hard worker

Are you ready to run a business?

Property investing is a fantastic business and a superb wealth creation tool, but be under no illusion that building and running your own portfolio is, first and foremost, a business and, like any other, a key part of it is all about balance sheets, profit and loss and cashflow. And for anyone looking at starting their own business, there's good and bad news.

The great news is that you're independent, you're working for yourself and not making profit to line anyone else's pocket. If you choose the right business and have a specific strategy in place, you can reach the first level of financial freedom - where you don't have to trade your time for money - relatively quickly. That, in turn, gives you more choices, and if you're leveraging other people's time, money and resources properly, you'll be getting richer even while you sleep. Doing all this, with the right values and conducting your business in an ethical way, will allow you to be more, do more, have more and give more and you'll find yourself tremendously successful and an inspiration to others.

The bad news is that the average millionaire has been bankrupt, or close to bankruptcy, three times before working out how to sustain their wealth (*source: Brian Tracy*). A very tiny minority are just naturally wired for success - they have the right beliefs, skills and personalities, select the right opportunities and are in the right place at the right time. It seems they can't fail - people like Michael Dell and Bill Gates, who made their first million when they were very young and have never looked back. But these kinds of people are very much the exception to the rule, just highly unique characters that end up being wildly successful. For the vast majority there are going to be gaps, weaknesses and blind spots in terms of the process of becoming wealthy.

Having personally been wiped out once – not bankrupt, but pretty close to it – and having had a number of successful businesses, I found out the hard way the importance of making sure you have a solid foundation of business fundamentals in place. I can certainly attest to the fact that most highly successful businessmen and entrepreneurs have been wiped out at some point, and I have a lot of respect for those people, because you know that they will have a wisdom and experience that goes beyond that of someone who's only ever experienced success. They tend to make better mentors because they have overcome adversity and found solutions, and they can absolutely identify with the concerns and fears of people just starting out.

I can't stress enough the importance of understanding these business fundamentals - things like cashflow, how to manage staff, how to establish and keep good tax, bookkeeping and accounting records, how to sell, how to market, etc. There are just so many skills involved in running a property business, which has all the functions you would find in any other professional business, and you need to make sure you're prepared for it. (see Chapter 10)

Unlike the commonly held myth that there is just one fixed set of traits that makes people successful, I subscribe to the belief that many different types of people can achieve success, as long as they are working in a role and a business that suits their natural strengths and talents. A very comprehensive study of some of the world's leading entrepreneurs, undertaken by Roger Hamilton and his team at Wealth Dynamics, has clearly demonstrated that success and wealth creation have been achieved by a very diverse group of individuals. However, what they have in common is the fact that they play to their strengths in an arena that rewards them handsomely for their performance. You can find out what your own wealth profile is by going to www.platinumpropertypartners.net/freeresources and accessing the Wealth Dynamics online test (there is a charge for this, which is lodged by Wealth Dynamics). This will help you better understand not only how to make the most of your talents, but also what types of people you need to find to help you overcome your weaknesses. Another useful tool you can access from the PPP resources page is the entrepreneurial profiler designed by former Dragons' Den panelist, Rachel Elnaugh. The free test only takes 15 minutes and it will show you what type of entrepreneur you are and what this means for you.

Some other relevant business statistics you should be aware of...

#1: Around 95% of business owners earn less than £50k per annum. They work an average of 12 hours a day, 6 days a week, and they earn less than they would get if they were employed and on a salary. There's a serious fact here that needs to be considered, because it's apparent that for the vast majority of self-employed people, being their own boss carries a premium and a value that makes the extra time and effort put in worth sacrificing an amount of income. And whilst being an entrepreneur and having financial freedom is a great aspiration for many people, the statistics waged against you in terms of significant success are pretty high. So how can you best stack the odds in your favour? For me, it's simple: choose a mentor or mentors who have been there and done it. It's worked for me in my past and I've been doing the same for others for many years now.

"The concept of 'Standing on the Shoulders of Giants' is believed to date back to the 11th century, and certainly, in my experience, the most sensible way to minimise the risk in setting out to achieve any goal is to find someone who has achieved what you want to achieve and learn directly from them."

Caroline Marsh,
Property Investor and C4 'Secret Millionaire'

For some people, their ego and pride gets in the way. This is more true for men than for women - it's the same reason men don't like to ask for directions when they get lost! - and it only makes sense if you are happy being on a slow path to success, as opposed to the fast-track.

#2: Around 90% of businesses fail within the first two years, and lack of adequate cashflow is the primary reason. Most people are over-optimistic, and there's a good rule of thumb in business that whatever your forecasts are, they typically take twice as long and cost twice as much to actually achieve. So one bit of advice I'd give people is whatever you think it's going to cost you and however long you think it's going to take, double both.

What's interesting - backing up the principle of mentoring and 'standing on the shoulders of giants' - is, if you look at franchising, that statistic is reversed. 94% of franchises succeed and are still going two years on and not only that, 90% of them are also profitable (source: NatWest/bfa Annual Franchise Report, 2009).

Now that's a strategic decision you need to make: whether to go it alone and have a high chance of failure, or actually buy into some kind of proven system with a much higher probability of success. I'd strongly recommend the latter.

#3: They say it takes a minimum of 10,000 hours and 7 years of dedicated effort, consistent learning and improvement to become a master in your field. Those figures came from studies on people who are masters in sports, business and music, and show that the primary driver for great success has to be a burning desire for whatever it is that being an entrepreneur or self-employed person will give you *(source: 'Outliers' by Malcolm Gladwell)*.

I would say that the key driver for the hundreds of people I've met and worked with is a combination of security and freedom. I was probably one of the worst employees in the world because I value my freedom, I like variety, and I don't like being told what to do by people I have very little respect for. I think, ultimately, success comes down to a combination of having the desire, the motivation and some burning ambition, and making sure your business and the people you work with are aligned with your values.

Every individual has a set of values, whether you're consciously aware of what they are or not. They are one of the things that fundamentally drive your behaviour. If you value variety and independence, then your chances of being successful in your own business are likely to be higher than someone who is actually quite comfortable being an employee and working for someone else who pays their wages. And if you're an employee who's been made redundant and forced into a situation where you have to consider starting your own property business, then you're going to have a different approach to someone who's taken the deliberate step to become self-employed because of their values and key drivers.

Whatever kind of person you are, it can be a long and rocky road to creating a highly profitable property portfolio. Whether you're just starting out or have already got a portfolio that may not be performing as well as it could, this book is intended to give you a helping hand. In the following chapters I'll be highlighting some of the key mistakes investors make and looking at how you can:

- Maximise your income
- Minimise your risks
- Get the best return on your capital
- Build a balanced portfolio that will bring you high returns
- Achieve long term financial security
- Systemise your business so you can spend more time working 'on it' instead of 'in it'

Preparation - Summary

- Be clear about why you're investing.
- Set timescales.
- Have written lifestyle and financial goals.
- Create your own vision board and encourage your family to do the same.
- Decide how much time you're willing and able to commit to your property business.
- Ideally have a minimum of £100k behind you.
- Become comfortable with the idea of risk and debt.
- Read and learn about successful people and what drives them, and apply what you learn.
- Visit our website, www.platinumpropertypartners. net/freeresources. Take the Wealth Dynamics wealth profile test and use Rachel Elnaugh's free entrepreneurial profiler.

Chapter 3

Mistake #1 - Not Protecting your Downside: Underestimating the Importance of Cashflow

"You only learn who has been swimming naked when the tide goes out."
- Warren Buffett
(source: New York Times, 1/3/08)

Shortly after the credit crunch ball was set rolling, with the collapse of Northern Rock in the late summer of 2007, we were exhibiting as Platinum Property Partners at the UK's largest property investment show, at London's ExCeL. The original topic for their panel debate had been scrapped and replaced with one asking what the credit crunch meant for the short to medium term future of the property market. The experts on hand – professional investors, owners of mentoring and investor training companies, legal and financial experts – came to the conclusion that this was a blip, a small correction, which would right itself in a year or so.

More than two years on, the reality has proved quite different, and several of the property investment companies who were at that show have since gone out of business. While I was also one of those trying to reassure people that property was, and always will be, a good investment, it wasn't because I'm an expert on economics or the financial markets and I had predicted the credit crunch. It was because I knew that a business model founded on the solid principles of strong income and profit and a best in class service is one that can weather pretty much any property storm. One of the key mistakes that's made time and time again by investors, is basing their business on something that works today, but is not future-proof. They see an opportunity in the market and put all their eggs in that basket. Great while the market conditions stay the same, but what happens when they change and 'the tide goes out'? Far too make people get caught swimming naked.

In the 10 years from the mid '90s, you didn't need to have much business skill to be a 'professional' property investor. The market rose so quickly and consistently that rapid capital growth was considered a sure thing. People soon started to rely on their properties appreciating at such a rate that every two or three years they could remortgage or sell properties they had developed and use the proceeds to either reinvest, or subsidise their salaries and improve their lifestyle. In both cases, everyone was lulled into a false sense of security and given an unrealistic idea of their own income. Affordability wasn't an issue: professional investors had a constant stream of capital they could access for deposit funds, and very few people chose to save for holidays or home improvements, they just remortgaged or sold properties.

The lure of property as a 'quick and easy' money making machine also attracted too many people who assumed this profit could be made effortlessly. Buy to let properties tended to be rented out to families, couples or individuals as single units, minimising the amount of hassle for the investor. Many were handed over to agents to manage, the rent covered all the costs, and if there wasn't much left over, or the investor had to throw in a little each month to keep things ticking over, it wasn't an issue, because the asset itself was scampering up in value and would periodically give a delicious lump sum payment. High tide and everyone's happy.

While there are many ways to make money from property, I am a firm believer in and promoter of having long term buy to let investments that are highly cashflow positive, as a solid foundation to a professional investor's business. This book, therefore, talks far more about this approach than 'buy to sell', property development or other investment strategies. Although 'buy to sell' and property development can both be profitable, you are only ever as good as your last deal and the profit it has made you. As a 'property trader/developer', as opposed to a long-term buy to let investor, your risks are increased, therefore these strategies should only be used if your wealth profile shows that you are better suited to being a property trader, or if you have already mastered profitable buy to let investing and are ready for a new challenge to diversify your investments.

The Downside...

There are probably three major external factors that can impact a buy to let property investor's portfolio and threaten their business:

1. Interest rate rises pushing up monthly mortgage payments.

2. A property market crash taking away the option of remortgaging or selling for a profit.
3. Void periods, where the units are un-tenanted and there's little or no rent coming in.

As a buy to let investor, you need cashflow. An interest rate rise puts a dent in your profit, and if you're unable to remortgage because there's no capital appreciation or loan to value rates have dropped, having monthly cashflow is the only thing that can keep your business profitable. If your tenant leaves and you have a month or two with nothing coming into the business, that's a serious problem, because you've still somehow got to fund the mortgage and any monthly bills.

'CASHFLOW IS KING!'

Many years ago, I found out the hard way that if you don't have cashflow, you don't have a business, and that's a lesson that's since been learned the hard way by far too many people. A lot of investors' entire business model, prior to the credit crunch, was focused on capital appreciation. While the long-term viability and profitability in property investing as a business is unquestionable, once that short-term capital gain was taken away, many buy to let investors and developers were ruined. A lack of available finance compounded the issue.

For example, one couple I spoke to in mid-2008 had a portfolio of 20 new-build apartments and small houses which were originally running at an average of £100 a month gross profit. The properties had all been expected to rise quickly in value but in fact had become a massive millstone round their necks that was cash-negative to the tune of £3,000 a month, with serious negative equity. The ways out of a situation like that are not attractive:

- Keep subsidising the portfolio, if possible, in the vain hope that it will recover.
- Try to sell the properties, but accept that the sale price will probably be below the amount owed on the mortgage and therefore a top-up will need to be paid to the lender.
- Default on the mortgage and allow the properties to be repossessed, which will result in a bad credit rating and the likelihood that getting another mortgage or any kind of credit will be impossible for a number of years.

The first two options depend on an investor having a serious amount of capital that they're prepared to lose, the third is, unfortunately, the only option available to most people. So how can you be as sure as possible that you never find yourself in that position?

When I moved into investing in residential property seriously, having had two businesses more-or-less wiped out, I was determined to make sure that the potential downsides in my new property business were covered, long term. Capital appreciation is a fact, not a 'strategy'. It's nice to be able to remortgage as and when possible and know that your long-term future is secure, but if property was going to be my primary business, I knew it had to be profitable *today*, i.e. generating a consistent, reliable and secure monthly profit.

Your biggest asset

Ask people what their biggest asset is and most will reply, "My home", but 9 times out of 10 they're wrong. What they're not thinking about – and I'll freely admit it's something that I didn't really consider myself until I started professionally investing – is that property is only a true asset to you if it's servicing its own debt. If you have a mortgage and use part of your salary to pay it every month, the slightly uncomfortable reality is that your home is probably your biggest liability.

And that's just a fact of life isn't it – we work to service our cost of living? That's certainly the traditional way of looking at life, and the majority of people do go to work every day to pay the monthly bills. But the whole underlying principle of your business life should be to create passive income – establish streams of revenue which cover your monthly outgoings and continue regardless of whether you are there or not, i.e. you're not trading your time for money. Property can be the main income stream for you. I make sure that every buy to let property I or my partners buy is truly an 'asset'. It must not only service its own debt, but also bring in a high enough level of profit that we can draw an income and are very well insulated against market fluctuations and interest rate rises.

Achieving such significant cashflow from properties is fairly straightforward: it's simple, but it's certainly not easy.

The people who thought their fortune was there on a plate and they could get very rich for relatively little effort are the people who are floundering now. Be under no illusion that what I'm coming on to talk about is not a 'get rich quick' strategy - it's a 'get very rich, steadily' approach – and it does require effort, particularly for the first couple of years.

Achieving high cashflow to protect your 'downside'

I'll cut to the chase: by far the best and most reliable way to maximise your rental income and profit from a property is to invest in Houses in Multiple Occupation (HMOs), where a large house is divided up to provide accommodation for usually 5 or more individuals. A typical HMO I own in Bournemouth, for example, will be a 4 bedroom, 3 reception room family home, which has been divided up as 6 individually let bedrooms, one communal reception room, a kitchen and two bathrooms – or, if the property allows, several en-suite bedrooms. HMOs have something of a seedy reputation and the assumption tends to be that they're low-budget student accommodation, house people on income support or represent 'doss-houses' for immigrants. The truth is, yes, there are lots of those out there, but providing low-grade, cheap accommodation is not what I recommend.

If you want to attract the best tenants who will pay the highest rent, you need to put in some effort and make sure you're offering high quality housing. There is huge demand in most parts of the country from young working adults looking for somewhere equivalent in standard to a home or a decent hotel, and that demand is growing. If you've seen the TV programme 'Friends', it's that kind of set-up: twenty-somethings, all with their own bedrooms, sharing the other facilities. Today's discerning housesharers also expect a cleaner and broadband to be provided, and if you can meet a certain standard and treat the people living in your house in a decent way, you should find they will behave decently in return.

We have Franchise Partners spread across the country who have houses full of great tenants. But there's still a way to go before the general population loosens up on its preconception that HMOs equal louts and layabouts who cause endless trouble for landlords and the neighbourhood. One of our Franchise Partners who is investing in HMOs in Gloucestershire is a very respectable man and operating entirely 'by the book'. But still, shortly after he'd completed on an early purchase, the neighbours complained to the council and even got a story published in the local paper, shrieking that he was going to lower the tone of the neighbourhood and create a dangerous environment by turning houses into drug dens!

That was an extreme case, but there can be a great deal of suspicion and objection that you may come across and need to overcome. Our 'drugs baron' (as we jokingly call him now!) has since received apologies from most of those neighbours who complained, some of whom have openly admitted that the kind of young working people he has renting rooms are actually no trouble at all, and conceded that they're probably less trouble than a 'normal' family with teenage children might have been.

The majority of people I speak to are quick to say that

they don't want to get involved with lots of tenants because of the amount of hassle they create, especially phone calls at all hours about blocked toilets. The truth is that yes, there will be some problems, but the huge upside is you're benefiting from 2 to 4 times the level of rental income you would have got from letting the property as a single unit. Done in the right way, it's a system you can hand over to someone else who you can employ to manage your portfolio.

Good, recession-proof income

Acknowledging there's work to be done, when you look at the figures, everything gets put into perspective. Operating these kind of multi-tenanted, professional let properties, which we'll look at more closely in due course, should mean a profit of around £12,000 per annum, per property for you. Now, you can't expect to do nothing for £1,000 a month profit, and if you set up and run your business in the right way, as your portfolio grows you will be able to afford to take on a part-time and then full-time property manager to handle all this for you, at which point all that should be required of you is a few hours a week. Your cash-positive HMO portfolio becomes your almost passive, leveraged and primary source of income. Our very first Franchise Partner followed this model and now employs a number of people to help him in his business.

The reason for making such an effort with HMOs comes down to protecting your downside. You tend to break even or run a very small profit by letting a property as a single unit or handing the entire letting and management of it over to an agency. The smaller your profit margins, the more exposed you are, and the more vulnerable when shifts in the property and mortgage markets occur.

By letting 5 or more individual rooms in a property, you will roughly double – and could even triple - the income you would have got from letting it to one tenant, and the added bonus is the likelihood of having a whole property vacant at any time is virtually nil. Rooms 1 to 4 tend to cover your mortgage and bills, and then rooms 5 onwards are more or less your profit. Professionals in this sector of the market, like our Franchise Partners, operate at a minimum of 97% occupancy most of the time. This is because if one room out of six is empty, it only has a $1/6^{th}$ of an impact on occupancy, compared with a single let which is 100% empty.

For too long, people have been fed the idea that they can get rich and stay rich through property investing, with no money, no skill and no effort, and it's simply not true. HMOs require hard work and a solid strategy behind them, and it's not a market for amateurs, but if you're prepared for that, you'll end up with a solid, virtually recession-proof income.

As I've indicated, it's not an easy route to go down and I can't stress enough the importance of spending time talking to people who make their living from this kind of investing, because it can be a minefield. There are a huge number of legislative issues governing what can and can't be done, and if you're not even aware of what questions you should be asking, who you should be asking, and what answers you're looking for, you can get in a serious mess. But assuming you're working with the right people, are prepared to put in some hard work at the start and are adequately funded, there are potentially great rewards.

Case Study

Here is an example of a highly cash-positive HMO bought by a PPP Franchise Partner in 2008:

Purchase Price	£225,000
Mortgage at 75% LTV	£168,750
CAPITAL INVESTMENT	
Deposit of 25%	£56,250
Refurbishment & all purchase costs	£54,000
Initial Capital Invested	**£110,250**
EQUITY RELEASE AFTER 6 MONTHS	
Post-Refurbished Value	£300,000
Further Advance/Equity released (75%)	**£56,250**
Capital/Equity left in property	**£54,000**
PROFIT AND LOSS	
Annual Rental Income	£46,800
Annual Costs (mortgage, etc)	£28,480
Annual Gross Profit	**£18,320**
Annual Return on Capital	**33.9%**

The gross profit figure has been calculated as a minimum and can be elevated with things like laundry income and by having double occupancy in one or two of the rooms, subject to obtaining any necessary permissions from the local council. There are other variables which are outside your control, chiefly interest rates and maximum loan to value (LTV) levels, but the beauty of this model is that if interest rates fall, your cashflow increases, and if they rise you are very well insulated because of the high level of profit you're making.

When the feeling in the market is that interest rates may rise, you should aim to secure a 3 to 5 year fixed mortgage option, so that you can keep better control of your monthly outgoings. With a lower LTV your capital input is going to be higher, but your cashflow better, and as time passes and you're able to re-mortgage, you should eventually be able to release all your capital and still reap a good monthly profit, giving you an infinite return on your investment.

These kind of properties are refurbished to a high standard and attention is paid to providing exactly what the 'young professional' market is looking for, so we are able to charge the top rents in the area. Here are photographs of the accommodation in some of our Franchise Partners' properties:

Because the Platinum Property Partners HMOs give this great level of security and superb potential returns, a lot of buy to let investors are seeing them as a 'silver bullet' to solve their lack of cashflow problems. Some realise they can adapt properties in their portfolios and turn them around from being cash-negative – but while it's a simple concept, it's not an easy strategy to implement correctly. In far too many cases, landlords are either unaware of the potential pitfalls or simply gloss over them, and rather than protecting their downside, they end up falling foul of the law and local council planning, building and HMO regulations. This can result in large fines, not to mention the huge costs that can be incurred in retrospectively ensuring a property conforms to requirements.

Putting things right retrospectively is far more expensive and time-consuming than getting it right first time and sometimes it is impossible, leading to dire consequences for the investor. Landlords who haven't been dealing with this sector for the past couple of years are often unaware of recent and ongoing changes in legislation. There are specific ways to advertise, to ensure you get the best response from prospective tenants, and then managing those tenants and the property is yet another string to the HMO bow. Successfully managing an HMO portfolio is a fairly complex business and to thrive and grow you need to be highly professional in your approach.

It might sound as though I'm trying to put you off, and in a way I suppose I am. Unless you've looked at all the potential downsides to operating this business model and are certain you can deal with them effectively, you'd probably be better not taking this path. But if you are sure, then I absolutely believe that HMOs provide the perfect foundation to a property portfolio, and please be reassured that with the right advice and support, there are solutions to nearly all challenges.

To give you an idea of the types of areas and topics you need to set up and manage if you are considering following the HMO model, here is a list of some of the contents from just one of the Platinum Property Partners Operating Manuals:

PREMISES and EQUIPMENT

PREMISES
OFFICE SPACE

OFFICE EQUIPMENT
FURNITURE
STATIONERY
FILING SYSTEMS

TELECOMMUNICATIONS
TELEPHONES
> Supply of telephone services
> '0845' numbers

TELEPHONE ANSWERING MACHINE
FAX MACHINES
ADSL / BROADBAND

COMPUTER EQUIPMENT
HARDWARE
> PC Specification
> Printer
> Pricing

SOFTWARE
> Operating system
> 'Office' suite
> Firewall and virus protection
> Web browser and email
> Data back up software
> Google Earth

SUPPORT / MAINTENANCE SERVICE
> Computer
> Printer
> Data Backups

VEHICLE
SUITABILITY
CLEANING AND MAINTENANCE

PROPERTY ACQUISITION

SOURCING PROPERTIES
ESTATE AGENTS
INTERNET
PPP PROPERTY INVESTMENT LOCATION ANALYSER
      Right Move / Spareroom / Easyroommate etc
      Newspaper advertisement
      Responses to advertisements
      Other landlords
PPP PURCHASE AND RENTAL PRICES SPREADSHEET

DEAL ANALYSIS
ANALYSING THE VIABILITY OF PROPERTIES
SUMMARY OF PROPERTIES
THE HMO ANALYSIS TOOL
      'Rules of thumb'
      Non mortgage funding

VIEWING PROPERTIES
BOOKING VIEWINGS
      Estate Agent relationships

BUYING A PROPERTY
MAKING AN OFFER
      Property Analysis ratios
      Emotional detachment
      Using the correct terms
SALE AGREED
      Managing the sale
      Informing the broker
      Instructing the solicitor
      Instructing the surveyor
PROPERTY INSURANCE

EXCHANGE OF CONTRACTS

REFURBISHMENT

PREPARING PROPERTIES
STANDARDS
>Legal and regulatory requirements
>Security Services
>Décor
>Fixtures, fittings and furnishings
>Utensils and appliances

COSTING PROJECTS
THE PPP REFURBISHMENT PROJECT COST SHEET
COSTS AND ECONOMIES
>Under-spending
>Over-spending
>Property standards reviews

PLANNING CONSENTS AND BUILDING REGULATIONS
PLANNING PERMISSION
>Change of use
BUILDING REGULATIONS
HMO LICENSING

CONTRACTING THE WORK
FINDING GOOD CONTRACTORS
KEEPING GOOD CONTRACTORS
OBTAINING QUOTES
>Estimates
PAYMENTS

PROJECT MANAGEMENT

SITE MEETINGS

> Changes and amendments
>
> Stage payments

COMPLETION OF THE WORKS

SIGN OFF AND SNAGGING

> Contractor relations

TENANTS

FINAL ARRANGEMENTS

UTILITY BILLS

REDIRECTING MAIL

LETTINGS and MANAGEMENT

MARKETING AND LETTING

FINDING TENANTS

MARKETING AND ADVERTISING

> Newspaper Goldmine advert
>
> Websites
>
> Word of mouth
>
> Existing tenants
>
> Estate agents/Letting agents
>
> Local major employers
>
> Signboards
>
> Postcards in newsagent's windows
>
> Local hospitals
>
> Recruitment agencies
>
> Leaflet drops
>
> Local tradesmen
>
> Ethnic groups
>
> Local Business Associations

RECEIVING ENQUIRIES
>Call Enquiry Sheet
>The PPP Property Investment Location Analyser

ASSESSING TENANTS
VIEWINGS / SHOWROUNDS
>Personal security
>Declining enquirers

NEW TENANTS
TAKING DEPOSITS
INFORMATION PACKS
>Photocopying records
REFERENCES
SIGNING THE AGREEMENT
TENANT MOVE IN
>Inventory check
>Defects
>Keys
>'Personal details'
DEPOSIT AND RENT PAYMENTS
>Tenancy Deposit Scheme
>Rent payment intervals
>Cash rent collections

TENANT ADMINISTRATION
ADMINISTRATION CHARGES
NON-PAYMENTS OF RENT AND CHARGES
GUESTS
PERSONAL RELATIONS WITH TENANTS
HOUSE RULES

TENANTS LEAVING
TENANT GIVES NOTICE TO QUIT

SERVICE STANDARDS

ABOUT CUSTOMERS

ESSENTIAL GOOD PRACTICE
OFFICE
VISITS /SHOW AROUNDS
TAKING MESSAGES
CUSTOMER CONTACT

CUSTOMER CARE
KEEP SMILING

TELEPHONE TECHNIQUE
GOLDEN RULES
INCOMING CALLS
OUTGOING CALLS
TELEPHONE ANSWERING MACHINE MESSAGES

COMPLAINTS
DEALING WITH COMPLAINTS
HANDLING A COMPLAINT
RECORDING COMPLAINTS
REPORTING COMPLAINTS TO HEAD OFFICE

BUSINESS ADMINISTRATION

THE BUSINESS PLAN
CASH FLOW FORECAST
> Targets

ACCOUNTING AND BOOKKEEPING
ACCOUNTING AND BOOKKEEPING SYSTEMS

KEEPING FINANCIAL RECORDS
>Purchase invoices
>Sales invoices
>Cash Book.
>Petty cash
>Bank reconciliation

STATIONERY AND TELEPHONES
ORDERING STATIONERY
PPP MOBILE TELEPHONES

THIRD PARTY SUPPLIERS
OFFICE ADMINISTRATION
OFFICE HOURS
OFFICE DIARY
PROPERTY RECORD KEEPING
>Filing
ELECTRONIC RECORDS
>Tenant Rent Record Sheet
>Rent Roll and Tenant Information sheet
>Computer data back ups
KEY CONTROL
>'Suited keys'
TENANTS VACATING
>Availability details – white board
>Office procedure following vacation

TAXATION
INCOME TAX
VALUE ADDED TAX (VAT)

INSURANCE
PROPERTY RELATED INSURANCE
>Buildings Insurance

Contents insurance
BUSINESS RELATED INSURANCE
Alternative accommodation and / or loss of rent
Public Liability
Employers Liability
Terrorism cover
Legal Expenses Cover
Landlords' Tenancy Legal Costs
Properties which are unoccupied for significant periods
Landlords Rent Guarantee Insurance
GENERAL NOTES

REGULAR RETURNS
MANAGEMENT SERVICES FEE
ANNUAL ACCOUNTS

PAYMENTS AND RECONCILIATIONS
MANAGEMENT SERVICE FEES

STAFF
CONFIDENTIALITY

HEALTH and SAFETY
HEALTH AND SAFETY IN THE WORKPLACE
ACCIDENT BOOK
HMO HEALTH AND SAFETY

Protecting Your Downside - Summary

- Remember that cashflow is king.
- Capital growth is a given, over time – you need to concentrate on achieving monthly profits in order to keep your business liquid.
- Take excellent tax advice to minimise your liability.
- Make sure the properties in your portfolio are truly assets, i.e. paying their own debt and making profit on top.
- Be prepared to put in hard work and understand that you can't get something of value for nothing.
- If you have single-let properties, re-assess and see if they could work harder for you as HMOs.
- Don't attempt to enter the HMO market alone if you're a novice – spend some time and money investing in advice and mentoring from experts.

Chapter 4
Mistake #2 - Not Having
an Effective Property
Investment Strategy

In a nutshell, an effective investment strategy is all about following a proven, disciplined, well thought out plan, and it comes back down to you really seeing property investment as a business. Doing personal preparation and spending time understanding your own motivation, aims and goals is the first step, which will give you a framework for your strategy. Once you have an idea of what kind of investments you need to make in order to get the results you're looking for, you will be most effective if you follow tried, tested and proven systems.

Occam's Razor:

'The simplest solution
is usually the best'

I'm a great believer in the Occam's Razor principle, which can be expanded and applied to business like this: you have the greatest chance of success, in the fastest time, if you follow a model that you know works and learn from those who have already trodden the path. 'Stand on the shoulders of giants' and take advantage of the wonderful opportunity you have to avoid making the mistakes others have made.

'You don't know what you don't know'

Not acknowledging that old saying is probably the thing that loses people the most time and the most money. We are all, to a greater or lesser degree, 'unconsciously incompetent' in certain areas of business and life. We can't excel in something if we're unaware what excellence is, and that's why you should never stop learning, no matter how much you *think* you know about a subject.

I learn something new every day, and if there's just one piece of advice you take away from this book, I hope it's that you keep an open mind and never stop learning.

Here's a practical example of how 'unconscious incompetence' relates to property investment and can impact negatively on your business:

Return on Investment (ROI) is a fundamental of investing and one which you must understand. If you invest £40k in an HMO, which brings you £10k profit a year, that's a 25% return on investment (the profit, divided by the capital invested) - essentially, the investment will have paid you back in 4 years (excluding appreciation, tax, etc, for the purpose of keeping the example simple). If you only have £10k of your own money tied up and it's bringing you £10k profit a year, that's a 100% return. But if you have none of your own money in the deal, even if it's only bringing you £4k a year, that's an *infinite* return on investment - it's costing you nothing to reap the profit, because the entire investment is funded by leveraged finance: Other People's Money.

If you don't know that it's possible to get a 20% or 30% annual return on investment from a property, and your expectation is set at 5% or 10%, then you're never going to be as successful as you could be. Your lack of knowledge and understanding of not only *what* the potential returns are, but *how* to achieve those returns, means you're going to waste time and money trying to work out how to make greater profit.

I've given hundreds of presentations to investors and had individuals come up to me, look at some of the sample figures for an income-producing property portfolio and declare them 'impossible'. That arrogance - the assumption some people have that they know all there is to know about a subject, and they have nothing more to learn - is something I don't understand, because it's just self-destructive. If you don't believe it's possible to generate over £10,000 gross profit per property, per annum - after paying the mortgage and bills, making an allowance for voids, and factoring in the cost associated with the funds you have invested - and you're not prepared to take a little time to find out how it might be, then that will impact greatly on how successful you'll be. As at September 2009, our Franchise Partners are making an average of £12,500 per property, and this is so far proven in 36 locations around the UK.

You can't underestimate the importance of learning your strategies from people who have proven they know how to achieve the same things you want to achieve. Nobody gets things right first time – and rarely second or third time! Why wouldn't you take advantage of someone else's experience, benefiting from them having made and learned from the mistakes already for you? It's a short-cut to success and by far the smartest way forward. Too many people consider it a matter of pride that they succeed entirely on their own, and they may well succeed, but not before they've spent a number of years and a whole lot of money on their way to finding the best route to success. As I said earlier, the average millionaire is said to have lost most of their money around 3 times before they find a way to hold on to it. Why choose to go that route yourself when there are now so many opportunities to access their refined and proven strategies?

There are many ways to tap into this knowledge – books, training workshops, coaches and mentors, franchise businesses or linking up with business partners. You'll have to invest a little up front but in most cases it will pay you back many times over.

We regularly hold low cost workshops where we impart significant knowledge alongside leading industry experts and professional investors. To find out if you qualify for a free place at an upcoming Platinum Wealth Workshop, visit www.platinumpropertypartners.net/freeresources.

What can happen if you don't use a proven strategy...

We had some clients down in Brighton, who understood the huge benefit of working with professionals. They quickly built up a million pound plus portfolio, mostly acquired at below true market value, which had a gross profit of £50k per annum, from rental income alone. At around the same time, some close friends of theirs also decided to invest in property, but on their own. With the same amount of capital invested, they bought a £2m portfolio, which, on the surface, sounds impressive. What was far less impressive was that the portfolio declined in value by about 15% almost instantly, and was cashflow negative to the tune of about £60k per annum, with very little chance of capital growth in the short to medium term.

These friends had tried to avoid spending what they thought was a large amount of money on getting educated about an area in which they were 'unconsciously incompetent'. The result demonstrates how making poor investment decisions with no supporting effective strategy in place can cost people a huge amount of money. I could fill another book with similar stories of people who have done exactly the same. Making really fundamental errors early on, because they don't know what they don't know, can seriously mess up people's plans for their lives. Pensions and incomes can be ruined, and quality of life can suffer hugely as people have to work longer hours to compensate for their bad investment decisions.

Buying a property is not difficult – any idiot can do it – but buying a property that will meet and deliver on your financial objectives - whether that's high capital growth and/or great income - is a science. Yes, you *can* be successful in property on your own, gain financial independence and secure your future, but it might take you 20 years, and why spend 20 years when you can do it in 3, 4 or 5 years by standing on the shoulders of those who have gone before you?

The 'Holy Grail'

In the worldwide best-selling book, 'The E-myth Revisited', Michael Gerber defines 'the Holy Grail of business' as a prototype business model that can easily be replicated.

I'd expand on that simple franchising concept with something I learned from a very successful entrepreneur in the States - Larry Wilson - who's a consultant to some of America's leading companies and a very successful turnaround specialist. He says that if someone asks, "What do you want your business to achieve?", the answer should be "sustainable and profitable business growth"; i.e. you want your business to keep funding itself, keep growing and be profitable. This applies to a property business as much as any other.

And that's why property investment makes such sense: it can provide you with the perfect vehicle for a profitable and sustainable business, and you have the extra benefit of an appreciating asset. You're making money on an ongoing basis and the asset value is something you can refinance or sell at a later date, medium to long term, for a profit.

For me, property is the 'Holy Grail', quite simply because it can fulfil all the principles of a successful business model:

The 'Holy Grail' of Business:
'Sustainable and profitable business growth, with an appreciating underlying asset base and highly effective tax avoidance strategies in operation.'

There will be many different elements to your overall property investment strategy, but five of the key points to make sure you have covered are:

1. Ensuring your leveraged income exceeds your monthly expenses
2. Ensuring you have multiple streams of income
3. That you are able to recycle your capital
4. Minimising your tax liabilities
5. Your exit strategy/ies

Let's look at these in more detail.

1. Have your leveraged monthly income exceeding expenditure

This is what I define as 'the first level of financial freedom'. Your first major financial goal should be to get to the point where you don't have to trade your time for the income that covers your mortgage or rent, bills and general expenditure. That means you have to establish a business model which is not dependent on you for its daily running. It's a system which may be ultimately overseen by you, but it generates profit whether you're there or not.

An HMO portfolio can allow you to achieve that first level of financial freedom relatively quickly. In order to establish the kind of property business that is effective in delivering passive, leveraged income consistently, you need to ensure your business model is robust. And before you can do that, you need to make sure your financial blueprint

– the way you are programmed to *think* about and manage money – is aligned with success and wealth.

At this point I should say that if you haven't already read Robert Kiyosaki's 'Rich Dad, Poor Dad', make sure it's the very next book you read; I'll even forgive you putting this down to go and read it now! It is one of the most widely-read books in its field and is often referred to as the most successful financial book of all time. It addresses the proven fact that unless you make sure you think and behave like a rich person, you will never achieve long-term wealth.

One of the observations Kiyosaki makes is that most people earn an income from working and then use this money to live by paying for their expenses. This leads to the proverbial 'rat race' syndrome where people are forced to go out to work just to maintain their current standard of living. Kiyosaki asserts that wealthy people buy assets which generate income and their living expenses are covered by the proceeds of these assets. The enormous benefit to you of mastering and executing this approach is that it enables you to step off of life's rat race treadmill for good, so that you no longer have to trade your time for money.

2. Multiple Streams of Income

While HMOs can provide you with a very good income, which should become much more passive over time, your property business is at its most robust when you have a balanced portfolio. Every great entrepreneur understands the sense in having Multiple Streams of Income (MSIs), which can be different businesses and/or strands in the same business. The principle is that should one or two streams suffer at any point, the others will carry any shortfall and enable you to keep all your business interests running.

Imagine a diving board that's supported by one pillar at one end. When you put any force on the other end it's going to bend right down, collapsing if the downward force is too great. I use that as a metaphor for creating wealth: if you've only got one business and one source of income, and something bad happens to that, you're in big trouble. If the diving board is supported by multiple pillars it can withstand far more downward pressure. The same principle applies to your financial security.

In property, having MSIs generally means making investments which will bring different rewards at different times. I would guide most people to look primarily for an income-producing portfolio, so they can give up 'the day job', and while HMOs may be one part of that, there are a number of other options, e.g.:

- Sub-letting another investor's property, where you rent the premises from a 3rd party, sub-let at a higher rental level and profit from the difference.
- Managing other landlords' properties alongside your own. If you already have a property manager, you are simply adding to the portfolio they're managing, and increasing your income for very little (if any) extra cost.
- Lease options, which are similar to sub-letting, but rather than renting a property, you lease it for a specified time frame, with the option to purchase it at any point during that time, for a pre-determined price. In the meantime you can almost treat the property as your

own and maximise the rental profit, subject to having legally valid managed option contracts in place.

The UK property market can fluctuate in the short-term - as we have seen in 2007-9. This means there may be little likelihood of capital growth for a few years in most areas, so you also want to look for other options which will give periodical lump sum cash injections to your property business. That can come from a variety of different sources, e.g.:

- Investment overseas, in high-growth emerging markets, where you can get your capital and profit back in 2-3 years.
- Refurbish a property and sell on for a profit.
- Develop a property and sell for a profit.
- Planning gains – adding value to a plot/s by securing development rights.
- Adding value to commercial property by negotiating longer and more profitable leases, possibly through refurbishment.
- Sourcing properties and development opportunities for a finder's fee.
- Self-build – building a single personal residence and then subsequently selling or remortgaging to release some or all of the equity.

There are so many ways you can make money from property - both residential and commercial - each of which require specialist knowledge in order to get the best returns, both now and in the future. But as long as you take the right advice, you should find yourself with a varied, exciting and profitable property business.

3. Recycling your capital

High cashflow is great for ongoing income, but the true measure of the profitability of your business, and what will keep driving it forward, is ensuring that your return on capital is as high as possible. You should plan to use your own capital first and aim to recycle as much as possible by refinancing after 6 months. Become confident that you can identify and secure the most profitable opportunities that will allow you to achieve a good rate of return.

You may then want to look to offer solid business ventures to 3rd parties who will fund your investments in return. This principle is something you have to understand and really get to grips with, because at some point you will probably run out of your own investment capital. If you're serious about building a property portfolio, therefore, it's highly likely you'll need to attract a passive investor somewhere along the way. There are three reasons someone will choose to invest with you – whether they like and trust you as a person, your track record and proven ability to deliver results, and the return on capital and security you're offering.

The ultimate goal to aim for is ending up with none of your own money tied up in a property, but it's been much more difficult to achieve that in the last 12 months than pre-2008. The upside of investing in HMOs is their potential to give a substantial passive income; the downside is you may have to be prepared to tie up a fair amount of cash, certainly for 6-12 months. Historically, there were creative financing strategies that could reduce or even negate the need for capital input, as long as you were buying substantially below market value and had professional brokers, solicitors and bridging finance providers.

However, in the 2008/9 climate - with borrowing back down at 75% loan-to-value for buy to let mortgages, no facility to remortgage for at least 6 months, and some of the specialist buy to let lenders having pulled out of the market - the options are more limited. On the upside, while borrowing is down, that means your cashflow is higher, but remember that the over-riding principle behind your business should be to have as little of your own capital as possible in an investment, in order that you get the best possible return. However, if you are a novice investor you'll need your own cash to start with.

4. Minimising your tax liabilities

There are many reasons why property is such a great investment, not least of which is because of the smart and legal ways to avoid paying tax. I should say that I'm not against paying tax – after all, it is what funds the NHS, schools, roads, etc. – but why pay more than you need to? A big mistake that many investors make is not engaging a competent accountant, and if you don't have the right professional advice, you may find that over 40% of your hard earned money goes to the Chancellor of the Exchequer, which could otherwise be avoided. I personally suffered from this mistake and it cost me not only a lot of money but also valuable time trying to 'unpick' a situation that my accountant had created.

There are many simple and sophisticated ways of legally reducing the tax that you pay on profits that you make, so make sure that you choose an accountant who understands the specific business that you are in and that they have the right qualifications. Ask for references from their other clients that are in the same/similar business to you and bear in mind that this is certainly a situation where paying for the right advice is worth every penny. We work with some of the best tax advisers in the UK and overseas, who keep us and our Partners one step ahead of this constantly changing market.

5. Your exit strategy

Too many people embark on new business ventures without really focusing on the endgame – where they want to be, when, and how they're going to achieve the desired result in that timeframe. In property, too many people fail to consider their exit strategy. A prime example is the Spanish coastal holiday apartment market, which boomed in the early 2000s, as hoards of Brits threw their savings at what promised to be a high capital growth, great pension plan, with holiday benefits in the meantime. I'd say the majority of buyers were looking for the 'get rich quick' solution, assuming they could hold the apartments for 3 or 4 years, then sell for a whacking great profit and bank the cash for a happy retirement.

The problem was they were seduced by the relatively low purchase price, the sexy brochures and a slick sales pitch, and didn't look hard enough at the reliability of the investment. If the motivation for making the investment in the first place was the ability to dispose of it in 4 years, that's the part they should have focused on. To start with, they should have been asking how many other units had been purchased by investors with the same intentions as them, what the underlying growth drivers were, who the eventual buyers would be and how they would finance the purchase.

You need to do a lot of due diligence when you're investing in property, and it's also important not to be blinkered in your strategies – yes, have them, but be prepared to adapt, because the property market is not a rigid thing. Sensible investing is making sure you have options and exit strategies, and while, if you've got a highly cashflow-positive property, you're unlikely to ever want to sell it, the ideal position is that there's more than one way to make money from the investment. Make sure it stacks up well for income, but also look at what could be achieved in terms of lump-sum or multiple benefits...

For example, one of my buy to let houses is a very profitable, 8 bedroom HMO that also has quite a good plot, which has the potential to be split to provide for a small block of flats and a bungalow. Applying for planning permission will use a small proportion of the existing property's cashflow, but if planning is granted, it means I can sell the investment on for a very good lump-sum profit or develop the plot myself; if not, then I still have an investment that will continue to give me excellent monthly income.

A great investment will have multiple 'angles' for making a profit. These are the ones to look for and buy, but make sure you analyse the potential downsides before making your move.

Deciding on your Property Investment Strategies - Summary

- Determine what results you want and when.
- Accept you don't know what you don't know and find out what your 'blind spots' might be.
- Stand on the shoulders of giants: find people who have achieved what you want to achieve and work on having them as your mentor.
- Make sure the strategy you're following has proven results.
- Aim for a business model you can eventually work ON, not IN.
- Aim to build multiple streams of income.
- Work with strategies that enable you to recycle your capital so it stretches as far as possible and you get the best return on capital.
- Make sure you're happy with your exit strategies.
- Get great tax advisors and accountants and aim to make them your best friend!
- Never stop learning.

Chapter 5

Mistake #3 - Believing what you Hear, Read and See in the Media!

The thing to remember about the media is that the people who own newspapers are in the business of selling papers and advertising space, not news. For television channels, viewing figures are what it's about. In both cases, the headlines have got to be attention-grabbing, and the truth is that highly dramatic or bad news sells far better than good news or no news.

By the middle of 2008, emblazoned across the front pages and television headlines were supposed facts and figures about the number of homes being repossessed and the rate at which house prices were falling. You couldn't move for documentaries about people who'd been financially crippled by the unsound investments they'd made in the new build market. You could have been forgiven for thinking that half the population was about to be made homeless, every buy to let investor had been rendered penniless and property was the worst basket to be putting your eggs in, certainly for the foreseeable future.

In truth, yes, those speculative investors who had rushed into investments without doing their due diligence or paying enough attention to their return on capital and exit strategies found themselves in a lot of trouble. While that's a terrible situation for them, and not one to be taken lightly, it was probably a good wake-up call for the investment market as a whole.

Property is not a game, and the fact that there are companies that have profited over the past decade from essentially convincing people that it more or less is, is virtually criminal. If there's a silver lining to this cloud, it's that perhaps the population at large is now more aware of the potential downsides of investing impulsively and taking facts and figures at face value.

While this storm was crashing about the media, professional portfolio investors were - and still are, as I write - quietly getting on with making the most of probably the best opportunity in their lifetime to acquire property. Those 'in the know' realise that the time to buy is while prices are dropping and the headlines are at their most negative. If homeowners believe the value of their house is still going down and have no idea when it'll reach the bottom of the downward spiral, those who *have* to sell will be keen to do so as quickly as possible. If an investor can offer them a quick way out and bring an end to the stress of worrying about not being able to make mortgage payments, and take away the threat of repossession and bankruptcy, then it's surprising what a powerful negotiation tool that time pressure can translate into.

And that's another angle the media love to use to whip up public indignation: stories about how money-obsessed, mean-spirited property fat-cats are mercilessly taking advantage of poor people facing a future without the security of their own home. While I know for a fact that there *are* investors who systematically seek out vulnerable homeowners to essentially cheat them out of what their home is really worth, there are increasing numbers of decent professionals simply looking to find a win-win solution. They aim to end up with a profitable business asset at a price that reflects the speed and ease at which they can release the vendor from their highly stressful financial obligations. They'll be open and honest with the vendor about what the property is worth to them and why, and they'll be interested in exploring the best possible outcome for both parties.

A dangerous game

The media is a powerful animal and the reason I get annoyed when people start quoting headlines is that they can create their own truth. If people are consistently fed information that convinces them house prices are going down, people who'd quite like to move but don't *have* to, will sit tight. Nobody really wants to buy, because they don't want to find themselves in negative equity, so those who know they will *have* to sell - for whatever reason - at some point in the next year, all fling their homes on the market to try to get the best price while they still can. But with very few buyers, supply exceeds demand and prices fall - it's a self-fulfilling prophecy.

All that is great news for investors who want to get hold of property at a good price, but it doesn't do the market or the country any good to have such massive fluctuations, although the 'boom and bust' cycle is something that, historically, has always happened in both property and the stock market.

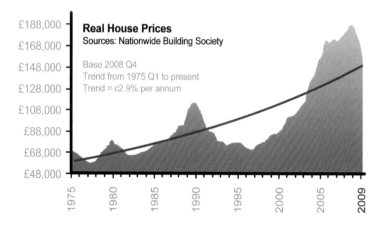

House price inflation, 1975-2009.

The other reason it's dangerous to believe everything you see and hear from the media is that headlines tend to represent the worst-case scenario, based on sweeping generalisations. Research is carried out, sources are quoted – Nationwide, Halifax, the Land Registry, the Department for Communities and Local Government, etc. – and they all sound terribly official, so we assume what they're reporting must be true. Of course they're not making up the figures, but it's easy to be 'blinded by science'. Just because an average figure has been calculated, and an interpretation broadcast, that doesn't mean it has the same meaning for you or that it's necessarily relevant to your situation.

For example, when the average house price in the UK is going down, the media usually focuses on it being a terrible thing that your home now isn't worth as much as it was last month. But if the market falls by 10%, and you're looking to move up the property ladder, that means although your home is worth 10% less, so is the one you're looking to buy:

can be selected or manipulated to support any number of theories and predictions.

On the 31st May 2007, the Daily Mail and Daily Express newspapers carried conflicting headlines - one warned of an imminent fall in house prices, the other reported the market was healthy and looked set to rise steadily for the foreseeable future - and yet both quoted the same source: the Land Registry.

In mid-July 2008, on Channel 4 news, the chief economist of 'Capital Economics' called property a 'snake' rather than a 'ladder', and said, "Don't touch property with a barge pole", predicting a fall in house prices of 40%-50% over the next 5 years. At the end of the month, the National Housing Federation directly contradicted that, predicting a rise in house prices of 25% over the same period, based on research by the independent economists, Oxford Economics.

So the next time you see a report about the housing market with an attention-grabbing headline and supporting statistics, just remember it may not be what it seems.

It's also important to understand that professional investing is a very different proposition to the residential housing market, where people are buying and selling their own homes. While the media might be crying out about it being a terrible time to buy, the truth is that there is no bad time to buy investment properties, provided you know what you're doing, employ a strategy that is suitable for the market conditions, and are taking the best advice.

The only bad time to buy property is 'later'!

Every market offers a different opportunity to make money, and the longer you delay taking action, the more of that opportunity you'll miss out on.

And it's not just the media you have to be wary of. If you're new to property investing or are about to embark on a new strategy, my first piece of advice would be not to tell anyone. At least try to avoid members of your friends and family who are likely to be unsupportive. They won't be able to stop themselves giving you advice, most of which is unlikely to be positive or encouraging. That's not because they want you to fail, but because some people – as with the media – have a tendency towards pessimism and to look at the worst case scenario, particularly when you're talking about new ventures.

The person who says it cannot be done should not interrupt the person doing it!

Just remember that if people aren't in the business themselves, they're probably basing most of what they're telling you on those good old media headlines and what they've heard on the grapevine. The Man In The Pub can't wait to give you 'advice' and tell you 'the reality', but it's rarely got any foundation, so do everything you can to avoid it - why subject yourself to negativity before you've started?

So if you can't trust what you read in the papers, and you shouldn't rely on friends, family or acquaintances to buoy you up, where do get advice from and whom do you trust? Well, rather than making the mistake of believing what you're told by those sources already around you, try actively seeking out success.

The best indicator that you are likely to succeed is if you emulate those with a track record. The first step is to identify some key people whose success, lifestyle and approach you admire. If possible, and if you know them, spend more time with these people. Be curious and ask questions, and see how you might be able to help them in return.

If the person you admire has a public profile, then read the books they have written and those they recommend; watch inspirational and motivational DVDs and go on carefully selected, recommended courses. You can even go into business with people to learn from them how to do business. Some of my best mentors have actually been business partners – they're not famous people or famous names, they've just been very inspirational in terms of what they have achieved.

To get an informed and balanced view of the property market and keep up to date with investment strategies that really work in the current climate, visit www. platinumpropertypartners.net/freeresources, download the 2009/10 Professional Property Investment Guide, and sign up to receive our free newsletter.

Mentors, coaches, trainers and consultants can all assist you in your development. You should be clear on the difference between them - the roles they play and their skill sets - and the following brief descriptions should help:

Coaching

The Chartered Institute of Personnel and Development defines 'coaching' as developing a person's skills and knowledge so that their job performance improves, hopefully leading to the achievement of organisational objectives. It targets high performance and improvement at work, although it may also have an impact on an individual's private life. It usually lasts for a short period and focuses on specific skills and goals.

A coach is somebody who has a skill set that's about helping you find the best solutions to challenges and problems you've got, but they won't actually have gone out and done what you want to do. You could have a coach for your property investing business who knows very little about property investing, but they're great at identifying and helping you work on areas of weakness.

Mentoring

Mentoring is traditionally associated with a more experienced person guiding and passing on their knowledge and experience to others. The mentee could be following in their mentor's footsteps, or using them as a role model. The modern twist to this is the 'reverse mentoring process'. This is a relationship in which a younger person has experience that they can share with the older generation - such as information technology. Essentially, mentoring is about sharing knowledge and experience.

A mentor is someone who has been there and done it, been through the school of hard knocks and achieved success in a way that you would like to replicate. In the case of property investment they will have made and lost money probably several times, worked out robust strategies and systems, tried numerous financing strategies and mastered the best, and they will have a solid portfolio which brings them income and will provide long-term financial security.

Training

Training is used when a skill - whether situational, theoretical or practical - needs to be taught. Examples of training-related activities include using new IT software, learning how to negotiate or learning how to do effective bookkeeping. The information is taught in a prescriptive mode.

Consultants

Consultants are used for the skills and experience that they can impart in a given situation. Consultants can give specific advice to an individual about the options available and the pros and cons of the choices they make. You hire a consultant to advise you how to go about a process.

I am where I am today largely because of the mentors and coaches I have had over the years. There's no way I would have been able to accelerate my success in the way I have without their training, guidance and support and I'm continually looking for people who can improve me and my businesses. I've worked with some very high achievers – Olympic gold medallists, billionaires, very successful property investors – and the overriding thing that comes across with all these men and women is that they are lifelong students. Whatever level they've reached, they know they can always improve and that there is something new to learn every day.

So don't be complacent, sit back and simply believe what you see and hear from supposedly reliable sources. Do your due diligence, question the information and be prepared to learn something that challenges what you might have believed up until that point.

> **'We remember 10% of what we read,**
> **20% of what we see and**
> **90% of what we experience.'**

This quote relates to Edgar Dale's 'Cone of Experience', which illustrates how effectively we absorb and retain information, i.e. learn. His research showed that the more actively engaged our senses are, the more likely we are to remember something, therefore books, DVDs and audio learning tools are only going to be a fraction as effective, long term, as actively experiencing and being physically involved. Here is a simplified version of Dale's original cone, first published in 1946 in his book, 'Audiovisual Methods in Teaching':

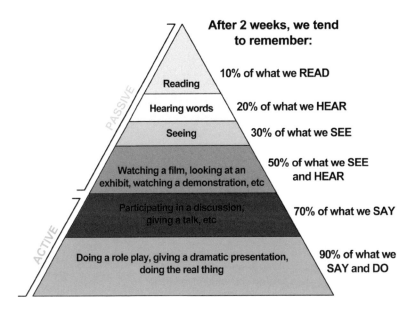

As the cone illustrates, don't underestimate the value in physically going out there and working alongside successful property entrepreneurs and businesspeople. I can give you the names of people I believe are the very best at what they do, and at the back of this book I've included a list of materials I think you'd get a lot out of, but ultimately you need to find coaches and mentors whose personalities and style fit with yours.

Once you start to surround yourself with successful people, you'll find that by adopting their attitude and approach, and following their core business principles, you'll start to become more successful yourself, I guarantee it. I was at a point in my life, about 10 years ago, when I suddenly realised that I was pretty much the most successful person in my social circle, and I wasn't moving forward at the same rate I had been. I made some changes, found some new mentors, in all sorts of different areas, and accelerated my own success again. It did mean that I lost a few friends/acquaintances along the way, and if you want to become truly successful, you have to be prepared to make some difficult choices about the people you spend the majority of your time with.

"Your Network equals your Net Worth."
- Mark Victor Hanson,
'Chicken Soup for the Soul'

Seek out good mentors, question what you hear and read and keep an open and inquisitive mind. Remember that the media is just a 'shop window' – you need to get behind the headlines and statistics and actively seek out the reality.

Not Believing Everything
in the Media - Summary

- Remember that the primary business of papers is to sell papers and advertising space.
- A great time to buy can be while the headlines are at their most negative and prices are falling, because when confidence is low, you have greater negotiating power.
- 'Boom and Bust' in property has historically happened every 15-20 years, so expect it to happen and plan for it, although timeframes do vary and the past will never be a totally accurate predictor for the future.
- Every area is its own micro-market – concentrate on the specific area/s where you're investing and the types of property that you want to buy.
- Surround yourself with those you want to emulate.
- Be a lifelong student.
- Your network = your net worth.

Chapter 6
Mistake #4 –
Not Operating with Integrity

"Integrity is doing the right thing,
even if nobody is watching."
- Unknown

I mentioned in the introduction that people have to like and want to work with you. I also talked about the importance of having a giving nature and an abundance mentality. Success in property, as in any other business, is about more than just treating others with respect and being personable, it's about integrity. If you lack integrity in your business dealings, you may win in the very short term, but it won't last in the long run.

Over the years I've seen people who have great drive and commitment to their business go bust because of the way they've done deals. Sometimes it's the foolishness of youth, but others believe it's clever to 'get one over' on the other party. They make a huge mistake by not appreciating the difference between sharp negotiation tactics and unethical business practice. Property is a business where, unfortunately, most of the key professions and players involved are stereotyped as being less than straight in their business dealings. We've all heard about agents taking backhanders from investors, gazumping, gazundering, vulnerable vendors being ripped off by unscrupulous buyers…the list goes on. If you're determined to make your way as an investor, it's doubly important you can stand up to scrutiny and reassure others that you're not only serious, but that they can trust you to conduct business with integrity.

I firmly believe that you sleep better at night knowing you have not had to tread on anyone to get to where you are, nor have you done anything that may come back to bite you.

Successful businesses are founded on successful relationships

The saying that your net worth is built on the strength of your network is absolutely true. If you want to gain access to the best deals and be able to move quickly and effectively in property investing, you need your 'power team' to be 100% behind you. On the legal and financial side you are employing these experts so they have a duty to you as their client and are obliged to act in your best interests. However, if you were to ask them to do things that fall into a 'grey' area, they would think you were trying to compromise their own integrity and wouldn't work for you.

If you're making repeat investments in a particular area, you need to have estate agents on your side, so be very careful, clear and up-front in your dealings with them. A lot of vendors are suspicious of investors and don't take them too seriously, partly because they think they'll make silly offers and partly because they worry that with no emotional attachment to the property, the investor might change their mind and pull out of the purchase. Some of those concerns are also shared by agents – and remember, they deal with 'timewasters' every day - so give them reasons to remember you as being genuine and build a relationship with them:

- Always try to register face to face with an agent, rather than over the phone, so they can get a feel for you and you, them.
- Show them you're serious by having all your information to hand when you register: most importantly your financial advisor/broker's information and details of your ability to finance purchases and move quickly.
- Always turn up to viewings and if the property's not right, explain why not and let the agent know what might make it work for you, or why it doesn't, so that they are better educated about your requirements for the future.
- Double-check your financial projections so you know where your maximum offer is, and make sure you can succinctly explain to the agent your reasoning.
- Once you've agreed a purchase, make sure you get the survey instructed as quickly as possible, to show commitment.
- Don't try to reduce your offer unless the survey gives you just cause.

In short, give agents every reason to pick up the phone to you first as soon as they value a property that might be suitable, and then recommend you to their vendor as a serious and reliable buyer. If you start messing about with the purchase price and back-tracking on negotiations, you'll quickly develop a reputation in the area and will miss out on some great opportunities. On the flip side, if you do what you say you're going to, when you say you'll do it, you should find agents very responsive over time.

To give you a case study, in early 2008 one of our PPP Franchise Partners agreed a purchase through an agent she'd viewed a number of properties with. She made sure she kept the agent updated throughout the transaction and dropped in a bottle of wine when she went to pick up the keys on completion. Later in the year, the agent rang her about a new instruction that she thought was an absolutely ideal investment; our Franchise Partner viewed the property without having seen any details, knowing the agent was reliable, and made an offer. Although it was below the asking price, the agent recommended that the vendor take it, knowing she could trust our Franchise Partner would complete the purchase as quickly as possible with no messing around. That's the kind of reputation you should be building with your business.

To continue the story, the purchase of that particular property went through relatively smoothly, in two months, but just before exchange it was suggested to our Franchise Partner by another investor that, as the market was still falling, she should try to negotiate £10k off the purchase price. She refused, saying she knew she'd already got a good deal and had shaken the vendor's hand at the agreed price, so going back on her word would be utterly wrong. Integrity is a trait that should run through everything you do. As well as giving others faith in you, you'll find that being able to look at yourself in the mirror and know you have done the right thing, morally and ethically, gives you a tremendous confidence boost when you go into new business negotiations.

In his widely acclaimed book 'The Millionaire Mind', Thomas J. Stanley discusses the results of a survey of US millionaires, which showed part of their psychological profile was:

"We became rich without compromising our integrity. In fact, we credit our integrity with significantly contributing to our success."

Warren Buffett, arguably the world's best investor, says in one of his books, "You can build your reputation for twenty years and lose it in five minutes", so you should never be greedy just to make an extra buck. He also says every transaction he's made seemed the best at the time and he never compromised his integrity in any of them. If you're looking to emulate successful people, following Warren Buffett's business principles is a very good start.

"When you choose to be pleasant and positive in the way you treat others, you have also chosen, in most cases, how you are going to be treated by others."
– Zig Ziglar

I personally believe that what goes around, comes around, and in the property world there are many examples of people who haven't acted with integrity and have had their come-uppance. To give you just one: on the South Coast, very close to where I live, there was a developer and entrepreneur who did pretty unscrupulous deals, focusing on buying large family homes, flattening them and putting up apartment blocks, much to the disgust of local residents. He swanned about on his yacht and made no secret of the fact that if people didn't like him, he didn't care. Because of the money he was making, he thought he was untouchable, but when the recession started to bite in mid-2008 his main company was completely wiped out, with millions of pounds worth of debts, and he was declared personally bankrupt in October 2008. This is the kind of person who would agree to buy a development site and then on the day of exchange would instruct his solicitor to tell the vendor he wouldn't proceed unless they knocked anywhere from £10k to £100k off the purchase price. Those types of practices create a bad reputation which in the end finds you out, and unethical behaviour will come back to bite you.

Another example of very common bad business practice is not paying suppliers on time, taking several months to settle invoices. That shows a lack of organisation, professionalism or cashflow and ultimately brings your trust into question. Nobody wants to do business with people they can't trust. As a property investor you tend to deal with lots of small businesses and sole traders, who often live month-to-month, so you should always make sure you pay them as soon as possible. These people are usually the tradesmen you or your property manager will need to call on at short notice, and they're far more likely to move quickly to fix problems if they know you always pay on time. If you do have cashflow problems, then inform your creditors and work out solutions with them as opposed to burying your head in the sand.

To give a personal example of operating with integrity, after Sept 11th, 2001, when I had to put a business I had into voluntary liquidation, my business partner and I decided to meet our key suppliers face to face and explain the situation to them. In all cases we found a win-win solution and in some cases, where they were small businesses that would have been seriously harmed if we had not paid what the company owed, we chose to make payments from our own personal funds, even though we were not legally obliged to do so. In other cases, some of the business owners accepted that our circumstances were out of our control and we agreed a win-win that did not involve us paying what the liquidated company owed but gave them some benefit moving forward. For example, promising to use them as a supplier in our other business but to pay 15% more than we were currently paying, until the amount owing was paid off, or proactively referring them new business and not taking a referral commission. In all cases, acting with integrity during that difficult time has been paid back to us many times over. On the back of that situation, we built a reputation as people who face up to problems and who do the right thing and it has led to long-standing, profitable and robust business relationships as well as a few great and enduring personal friendships.

"Try not to become a man of
success, but rather try to
become a man of value."
- Albert Einstein

The spirit of giving back

Back to the 'give more' principle. I find that when people have a spirit of wanting to share time, skills and money, it's a good sign that a relationship will be reciprocal and lasting. People who are naturally generous tend to have a high level of integrity in business. The flipside to that is a 'scarcity' mentality, where people feel there's not enough to go around so they play their cards very close to their chest. They keep their ideas and knowledge to themselves and will be very reluctant to share their contacts, experience and time, in the mistaken belief that they'll have an advantage over their peers and competitors.

In fact it's been proved that the more positive contacts you make with other successful people, the more your own success will grow – it's the old 'your network = your net worth' equation. A lack of integrity often goes hand in hand with a scarcity mentality and that's why those kinds of people might experience short-term success but it will more than likely disappear a few years down the line.

If you make a concerted effort to surround yourself with people who have an abundance mentality and show integrity in both their business and personal lives, you'll end up creating a powerful support network of like-minded people. That's the reason my partners and I created Platinum Property Partners. The thought of having long-term, win-win partnerships with an every growing team of like-minded, high net worth individuals was incredibly exciting. Now that we are much further down the line, it has proved far more enjoyable, beneficial and profitable for everyone involved than we could have hoped.

Always Operate with Integrity

- People do business with people they like and trust.
- Property is a people business and long-term success is reliant on a good reputation.
- Millionaires credit integrity with significantly contributing to their success.
- Have an 'abundance mentality'.

Here is a short story that nicely illustrates how lacking integrity will find you out in the end:

A lady walks into a butchers shop on Christmas Eve and asks for an 8lb turkey. The butcher only has one turkey left, which just so happens to weigh 8lbs so, smiling, he brings it out to the lady. Just as he puts it down on the counter, the lady remembers she may have a couple of extra guests coming, so she asked the butcher if he has a 10lb one.

The butcher sees he's about to lose the sale of this last turkey and suddenly has an idea. He takes it into the back room, rips off the 8lb weight sticker and replaces it with a 10lb one, lugs it back into the front of the shop and proudly puts it on the counter.

"There you go, a lovely 10lb turkey", he says.

"Oh, that's great," says the lady. "I tell you what, I'll take both!"

"Be more concerned with your character than your reputation, because your character is what you really are, whereas your reputation is merely what others think you are."
- John Wooden

Chapter 7

Mistake #5 - Not Maximizing the Potential of Leverage

"In the broad definition of the world, the word leverage simply means 'the ability to do more with less'."
– Robert Kiyosaki

In terms of investment, leverage is defined as 'the degree to which an investor or business is utilising borrowed money'; UK banks tend to refer to it as 'gearing'. It's also a key reason property is probably the world's greatest money-making machine. Ask a bank for a loan of £50,000 to invest in the stock market and they'll laugh you out of the building, but ask for £50,000 towards the purchase of a £100,000 property and the strong likelihood is they'll give it to you, subject to affordability and/or rental income. Property has always been, and will almost certainly continue to be considered one of the world's safest investment vehicles, and that's why institutions and individual passive investors are so willing to lend against it. And that willingness of 3rd parties to lend is what helps make me and you money.

Here is an example to demonstrate the power of leverage/gearing in property. If you already understand the concept, just skip over it, as I don't want to teach you to suck eggs!

- If you invest £100,000 of capital in the stock market, you have £100,000 worth of assets, and if the market

goes up by 10%, you make £10,000. That's a 10% return on investment.
- But if you use that same £100,000 to put down 25% deposits on buy to let properties, it gives you £400,000 worth of assets. And when the property market goes up by 10%, you make £40,000 – a 40% return – because you don't just profit from the growth on your own money, you also profit from the growth on the bank's money.

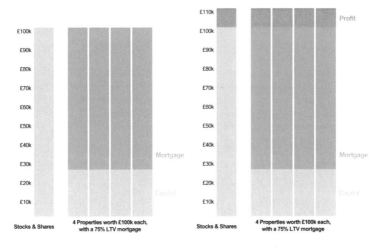

(The financial examples in this chapter are simplified and ignore purchase/sale costs, tax, etc.)

Leverage, or being highly geared, acts just like a magnifying glass. When the market moves upwards - and in your favour - leverage massively improves your returns. However, when we experience a market fall, a high level of debt can leave you exposed, especially if you do not have adequate profit margins built into your investment model. If you are going to gear up highly then using a robust, proven and very profitable model like PPP's HMO strategy is advisable. Failure to do this is what has caused thousands of highly geared investors to get repossessed in the last few years.

Good vs Bad Debt

The first step to feeling comfortable with debt is understanding the difference between good and bad debt. In property it comes down to ensuring you have assets, not liabilities. If, by incurring debt, you are creating an income stream – as is the case with highly cash-positive buy to let investing – that is good debt. The asset acquired should be not only covering the cost of servicing the debt (mortgage interest repayment) and any further associated costs (bills, tax etc.), it should be giving a healthy profit on top, and if that's the situation, you've got yourself some good debt!

Bed debt is the reverse - it means you have to pay out yourself to service it - so if you put a new music system on a credit card, for example, that's a bad debt. Not only does the product immediately depreciate, you also have to pay out interest every month.

In property terms, if you have to go to work to pay your mortgage, that is generally seen as bad debt. While capital appreciation will, over time, more than cover the interest you have to pay in the short-term, if you were to lose your job and stop paying your mortgage today, you would be homeless. Most people's home, if they have a mortgage on it, is therefore a liability.

The traditional way of thinking, and the philosophy most of us grew up with, is that your chief aim as a working adult should be to pay off your mortgage as soon as possible. Now, for those whose home is their only property investment, and who live pretty much month-to-month on their salaries, with no other income-producing investments, that's probably a good idea.

To know that you own your home outright and nobody can take it from you is a great comfort. But if you're serious about being business-minded and using property as an investment tool to create financial independence for you and your family, then owning a property outright is simply holding you back and is gross under-utilisation of your capital. As long as you are following a proven strategy, your quickest route to exponentially increasing your income is by leveraging borrowed finance.

In August 2007, when Amstrad's merger with BSkyB was announced, Sir Alan Sugar told The Sunday Times he was planning to turn his attention to his property portfolio, which he deeply regretted not spending more time on in the 'golden' 10 years from the mid-'90s:

"Throughout my career I have invested in property as security and seen the electronics as the risky part of my business. I've got £300m of property, mostly in trophy buildings around London, and I don't owe a penny. If this were leveraged properly it could be £3 billion overnight. I need to put these assets to work, raise equity and become a proper real-estate trader."

Sir Alan Sugar
(Source: The Sunday Times, 5th August 2007)

If it's taken Sir Alan all these years to appreciate the value of leverage, then you needn't feel too bad if the penny hadn't quite dropped for you until now either! What I would emphasise is the phrase in the middle of that quotation – "If this were leveraged *properly*..." – because it's imperative that you do your homework and have a solid plan for servicing the debt you'll be taking on, before you rush out and start looking to remortgage your home. Again, it's a simple principle, but not an easy strategy to execute.

Financial Freedom

This is the key motivation for the vast majority of property investors, and it means different things to everyone. For some, simply reaching the first level of financial freedom is enough, i.e. having your leveraged (passive) monthly income exceeding your monthly expenditure. So if your home mortgage payment, bills and all other outgoings add up to £4,000 a month, you need to be generating over £4,000 net income every month, from a source which doesn't require you to trade your time for that money. From a return on investment point of view, you need to have the income-generating asset financially leveraged as highly as possible, and you also need to be leveraging other people's time.

Case Study

Here's a real-life example of someone successfully using leverage in his property business:

Back in 2005, Neil Mansell was working in the City as a business development manager, earning £37,000 a year.

By using PPP's tried, tested and proven system, he bought his first PPP HMO in September of that year. Neil had been left some money by his grandparents and he used that for the deposit and other purchase costs. Once it was refurbished and rented out, that property gave him cashflow of over £700 a month, after the mortgage, all bills and other related expenses had been paid. Neil spent just over a year building up his property business part-time until, in January 2007, he was able to give up his city job and move into investing full time, as the income from his properties had matched his salary.

By the time he had bought his 6th property, Neil was in a position to be able to employ a property manager, allowing him to spend more time focusing on further acquisitions, incorporating different strategies and developing a diversified portfolio. It also gave him the opportunity to begin helping others, and Neil now mentors numerous clients around the UK, from first-time buyers to established investors. With this extra income, in addition to the income drawn from his portfolio, Neil earned well in excess of £100k in 2008, and he has now employed a few staff to support the running of the business which also allows him to delegate the tasks he doesn't enjoy and spend more time on those he does.

As at mid-2009, Neil's portfolio currently stands at over £3m in value, and his properties, together with other related income streams are bringing him an annual net profit of over £120,000. Through leveraging other people's time and money, Neil has built a business that makes him nearly four times what he would have been earning in paid employment and effectively achieved financial independence: he doesn't have to go to work every day to pay the bills.

The last three years have been hard work for Neil, but well worth it. The hardest part of the journey was taking the first step - realising that it was possible for him to achieve. The principle of utilising leverage flies in the face of what is fundamentally ingrained in most of us – that paid employment is a safe and solid option and debt is a bad thing. Just take another look at what Neil has achieved and start to appreciate that what most of us were taught when we were young was not necessarily right.

Spend your time doing *what* you want, *with whom* you want.

The point of all this – of working hard to maximise the benefit of leverage – is so that you can have more choices in your life. Most people talk about property as providing them with a secure pension, but do you really want to wait until you're retired to enjoy spending time and money doing something other than the 'daily grind'? Why wait until your 'twilight years' to do the things you actually want to do?

The 'new rules' are: *You* make the rules, and can shape your own financial future.

As I said earlier, one of the most important personality traits in all successful businesspeople is optimism and a belief that anything is possible, combined with a drive to work hard and never give up. A lot of people carry with them a belief that there is something negative about having a lot of money, that success in business implies too much personal sacrifice and a cut-throat attitude, and that while others might have wealth, they're probably not happy.

In my life I've chosen to take an average of three months' holiday a year to travel the world with my wife and children; I have a boat I regularly take out in the afternoons to go fishing with friends; I go to concerts, dinner parties and sporting events; I'm happy. I give to and support charities, and one of my greatest rewards in life is seeing people I've mentored achieve their desired quality of life, knowing I've helped them on their way. I'm saying all this not to impress you, but to impress upon you what is possible. Remember, I left school at 16 with no qualifications and very low self-confidence; I also lost everything I had at one point and had to start all over again. If I can create the life I want to live then I truly believe you can too.

People say money can't buy you happiness, but that's not strictly true. Money might not be able to buy friends or love, but it can give you a great deal of security, more choices and more freedom. Wealthy people can afford to give their children a lot of opportunities in life – they can have music lessons and sporting coaching; they can visit different countries and experience different cultures; if they're sick they can receive the best medical care; they have the freedom to choose what they consider the best schools for them, and they can live in a lovely home.

I have to say, I know and have met a lot of unhappy wealthy people as well as happy and fulfilled ones. This proves the fact that money doesn't equal happiness. However, ask youself this question: would you rather be poor and happy or rich and happy? Happiness and wealth are not mutually exclusive. When faced this kind of 'either/or' choice, most people will choose both - happy AND rich!

Back to the 'old rules' – the traditional assumption would have been that in order to afford all this, you'd have to be miserable, working all hours, ground down and stressed out. I work a lot because I love what I do. It's because I leverage other people's time and money to create my primary income streams that I can spend so much time away from 'the office'. If I was suddenly unable to work any more, I know that I've already put the pieces in place to not have to worry about my family's financial security.

Sure, there are still times I get stressed out – I take on too much, or things outside my control go wrong and need to be dealt with – but, on the whole, I am extremely blessed. And I take pleasure in helping others to have more choices, freedom and all-round success in their lives.

Leverage enables you to build a business which can essentially run without you, and it means your capital goes further. The more you earn, the more you can invest, and if you're leveraging correctly, your portfolio of assets will grow exponentially, as you use other people's money and time to increase your own wealth.

You need to get your head around good debt and understand that most of the richest people in the world built their wealth by firstly having huge amounts of debt. If you have any negative thoughts about what it means to be wealthy, get over them. Forget megalomaniac workaholics, the new wave of wealthy people are 'philanthropreneurs' – those who believe in sharing the wealth they create and making the world a better place. Paul Newman gave all the profits from his 'Newman's Own' range of foodstuffs to charity; Bill Gates has been funding medical advances in Third World countries for two decades. And remember, giving is not just about cash; you can give time, ideas, resources, etc.

Utilising leverage to create Multiple Streams of Income

Having multiple streams of income is a fundamental concept in leverage, but it does come with a health/wealth warning: don't start multiple businesses all at the same time! Early in my business building career I perfectly understood the sense in having MSIs: if one business is going through a difficult time, for whatever reason, your other businesses can carry you through. I was also (and still am) very ambitious and had great self-belief, so I started four different businesses within a 12 month period, thinking if anyone could build an empire, it was me. All that happened was that I worked far too hard, became increasingly stressed and ended up exiting from three of the businesses.

New business ventures require you to dedicate a significant amount of your time, energy and money in the early days, and you can't possibly build anything meaningful if your attention is split in a lot of different directions. The best approach is to have a Primary Source of Income (PSI) – the source that pays the bills and covers your basic needs – and then gradually build up other streams alongside it. If you correctly systemise your businesses and/or investments you'll find them easier to manage, then you can leverage other people's time and effort, freeing up your time to concentrate on creating yet more streams of income and investments.

The beauty of property investing is that your multiple streams of income can be all under the same umbrella, so a lot of your business support is probably already in place, making the 'start-up' easier. For example, if you have a few cash-positive buy to let properties up and running, you'll already have tradesmen and contractors – handyman, plumber, electrician, plasterer, painter etc. – so if you decide to move into self-build, you've got a head start on a network of people to do the work for you. If you move into international investments, you already have a good understanding of the financial aspects of investing and the administrative systems in place for keeping track of management information.

The key is not losing sight of your PSI, and ensuring it continues to hold up as a solid foundation for your other income streams. If your PSI is at risk or you don't enjoy it, then you have a big challenge to solve. Finding and growing a new PSI quickly is of paramount importance to you in this situation, so you need to act fast.

Utilise the Power of
Leverage – Summary

- Make sure you use leverage to acquire assets, not liabilities.
- Embrace the idea of 'good debt'.
- The first level of financial freedom is having your leveraged (passive) income exceeding your expenditure.
- Leveraging other people's time and money will allow you the freedom to choose how you spend your time.
- Think of leverage as an accelerant for your timescale to achieving your financial and personal goals.

Chapter 8

Mistake #6 - Not Investing in your own Personal and Professional Development.

"If you want to change the fruits,
you have to change the roots."
- T. Harv Eker,
'Secrets of the Millionaire Mind'

Ongoing personal and professional development is, without doubt, what will make the biggest difference in the level of success and financial freedom you achieve. In earlier chapters I've touched on different aspects of self-development; here I'm going to break it down into some core principles and theories, and give you tools you can use to improve how effectively you operate in key areas of business and life.

When I'm talking about our franchise business and people ask whether we give any guarantees the systems and methods we use will work for them, the answer is always no. I know the systems work – they're tried, tested and proven – but the vital variable we can't guarantee or control is the person operating the model. You might not have thought about it, but where you are in your life today is a direct reflection on how you've been operating in your personal and business life up until now. This means that if you're not as happy, successful, wealthy, healthy, fulfilled, etc. as you would like to be, then something fundamental needs to change.

"So where do I start?"

First of all, be clear in your own mind about what wealth, success and financial freedom mean for you. Everyone has a different vision for their future and, as with goals, which we'll look at more closely in Chapter 10, you have to know what you're striving for before you can expect to achieve it. What would it mean to you to be truly wealthy? What is your definition of financial freedom and what sum of money would you need each year to be financially free? There are different levels of financial freedom, so put some rungs on a mental ladder with price tags attached: the first level might be the amount you'd need to have in passive income to pay all your bills, essential expenses, holidays and a monthly allowance for new clothes and entertaining. Ultimately, most people aim to be completely debt-free, with more than enough passive income coming in each and every month, as well as a certain amount of capital at their disposal.

> **Be <u>specific</u> about *what* you want and *why* you want it!**

The more specific you can be about the amount of money you want and need to earn, the more likely you are to achieve that level of financial freedom. You also need to think about your motivation, which is often less to do with tangible targets that can be listed, and more about feelings and desires. What would financial freedom really mean to you and why do you want to be wealthy? Most wealthy people I have mentored appreciate the comfortable lifestyle money has afforded them, but what they really love is the freedom it's given them to provide opportunities and choices for themselves and, where applicable, their children. They can help other people who have less than they do and share their time and money, and they can choose to spend their time doing what they love with the people whose company they enjoy.

The stronger your desire to become wealthy for someone or something other than yourself, the more likely you are to achieve success and retain the wealth you create. One of our Franchise Partners had incredible obstacles put in her way, including being pulled out of school before she'd been able to sit her GCSEs and being widowed when she was only in her late 20s. Against the odds, she managed to create a small income from renting out part of her home, put herself through college, university and bar school, and is now, at 35, a successful lawyer and property investor. Her driver wasn't money, per se, it was her children and her focus was an absolute commitment to making sure their future opportunities and lifestyle weren't compromised by the loss of their father. That deep desire to succeed for the sake of people she loved and was responsible for, gave her an inner strength and the core belief that failure was not an option.

Success is a state of mind and a habit – as are mediocrity and failure! The great news is that it's within your power to change your financial and success blueprints so that they are aligned with where you want to be. You're in control!

But before you can kick-start your development, you need to:

Be AWARE you're out of balance
UNDERSTAND your challenges
and
Be WILLING and WANT to change

It has been proved that thoughts and beliefs lead to feelings, those feelings govern your actions and those actions lead to results. So start by asking yourself some questions about your beliefs surrounding success and money and remember that beliefs are not facts, they're simply strong opinions and that's why they can be changed. For example, what are your initial reactions to these statements?:

- Getting rich is down to luck or fate.
- If I make a lot of money I might lose it.
- Realistically, it would be difficult for me to get rich.
- I'm not clever or confident enough to get rich.
- Managing money isn't an issue because I hardly have any.
- If I make a lot of money, great, but if I don't, that's all right too.
- I'm too old/young to be rich.
- I'm not good with figures and managing money is a bore.

If you find yourself agreeing, even moderately with any of those, they could be limiting beliefs for you, making dents in your positivity and compromising your desire to become wealthy.

To receive a comprehensive questionnaire that will help you drill right through to the heart of any financial blocks and limiting beliefs you might have, visit www. platinumpropertypartners.net/freeresouces, where you can download the questionnaire and an action plan.

From now on, make a conscious effort to examine how you feel when you're talking about money or listening to other people discuss wealth, and also how you feel about seriously rich and successful people. I'm not saying there are specific right and wrong ways to think and feel, but you must be aware of your own reaction and if you have any negative feelings around wealth, they could be having a negative impact for you, personally. Write down any limiting beliefs you think you may have and then you can begin to address them.

---

4 great reasons to be rich!:

- Lifestyle – yours and your family's.
- The contribution you can make to others' lives – those close to you and in the wider world.
- For *who* you have to become in character and mindset – the satisfaction you will gain from your personal and professional development.
- Getting rich is proportionate to the problems you solve and the value you add to other people's lives – the richer you become, the more you will have positively affected others.

Think about how your parents and/or significant figures in your childhood thought about and treated money, and also about early experiences you had with money, because those are likely to hold the key to why you think and feel as you do. We either mirror or are entirely opposite to our parents, so you should be able to quickly see which you are. My father was careful with money – although he enjoyed gambling on the horses for fun, he only took calculated risks, based on a lot of research and form study. He always limited his bets and never gambled what he couldn't afford to lose. He also made sure he had savings, investments, paid off his mortgage and didn't buy impulsively. On the other hand, my mother loved spending – she was a little more creative and carefree in her attitude – which seemed to me a more fun way to be! We didn't have lots of new things, although we probably could have afforded more, so I grew up slightly resentful that I couldn't have many of the things I wanted. You'll see in a moment what impact the influences of my parents had in my life.

In her book, 'Money Harmony', Olivia Mellon states that there are four main money profiles: spender, saver, avoider and money monk. The first two are fairly self-explanatory. Avoiders just don't want to have to think about or deal with money, and money monks simply see money as beneath them and don't care about material things. You'll probably have a gut instinct about which you are – I was a natural spender – and if you're a combination, you'll find one will be your primary profile. Think about where your strengths and weaknesses lie, and what implications they have on your natural tendencies towards debt, money management, risk, and also on your feelings towards money.

SPENDERS

- Like to spend money, often linked with emotional happiness.
- Usually have low balances or are overdrawn on bank accounts.
- Have credit card debt.
- Usually impulsive and impatient.
- Believe they are spontaneous and generous.
- Tend to put off making financial provision for the future.

SAVERS

- Keep financial affairs in order and are good money managers.
- Are responsible and cautious with money.
- Tend to be risk-averse.
- Fear getting into debt and have little or no bad debt.

MONEY MONKS

- Believe money is beneath them.
- Bank account – what bank account?!
- Not interested in material things.
- Tend to be ungrounded and unstructured.

AVOIDERS

- Avoid responsibility for money and money management.
- Have lots of bills in a pile/drawer/shoebox!
- Procrastinators – put off dealing with money issues.
- Tend not to get stressed – 'ignorance is bliss' approach.
- Generally ignorant, irresponsible and poor.

Once you've identified which you are, you can then work to either balance yourself, or try to partner with people who are strong in areas where you might be weak, and vice versa.

A potential negative impact of a saver profile on wealth creation is that if you are naturally risk averse and fear debt, you might over-analyse deals and agonise over the financial implications, and it will take much longer to build your portfolio. You could even miss out on great deals because of your natural inclinations. Partnering or even just discussing opportunities with a spender will help balance your rationale. Conversely, a spender might be tempted to rush into deals without thinking through all the possible outcomes, and this is where a saver can help them.

Avoiders will never be wealthy, because you have to learn to manage money before you can hope to keep hold of it, so it's critical that they address what's causing them to behave in this way. As far as money monks are concerned, it's highly unlikely they would be reading this book in the first place! You should aim to be a healthy blend of saver and spender – willing to take on good debt and enjoying the wealth you create, while being responsible over money management and taking only considered risks.

When I first started to make good money in my late 20s, I enjoyed it. I spent a lot, Lucy and I had a lovely house, a great social life, I drove a nice car and I felt like I'd really made it. When I saw something I wanted to buy, my attitude was to buy it "because I can", and the result of that was that I went through money faster than I should have and didn't worry too much about investing seriously for the future. It wasn't until my two primary businesses were all but wiped out after 9/11, and the only thing that saved me was the equity in my home, that I realised something had to fundamentally change in my attitude. I found coaches and mentors to help me and I was able to change for the better – and you can too.

UNIVERSAL PRINCIPLES

- Until you can show you can handle what you've got, you won't get any more!
- The HABIT of managing money is more important than the AMOUNT.
- It's not: "When I have plenty of money I'll begin to manage it," it's "When I begin to manage it, I'll have plenty of money."

Making a change

Once you've identified your beliefs, why you hold them and which of them could be limiting and impacting negatively on your ability to create and sustain wealth, you can work on changing them. It's known as reconditioning, and there are a number of different approaches. I'd advise you to look into these in much greater detail. Working with coaches and mentors is great, but here are some illustrations of a couple of techniques that have worked and continue to work for me. Remember, keeping your mind on track is an ongoing project, not a 'one time' quick fix – these are processes, techniques and tools you should get in the habit of using.

> *"If you keep on doing what you've always done,*
> *you'll keep on getting what you've always got."*
> **- W. L. Bateman**

Pain versus Pleasure

The saying goes that pain causes change, and you'll find that while wanting a better life, financial freedom, security, holidays, etc. gives you some motivation to be more successful and create more wealth, you'll be even more motivated if there's a painful consequence of your not being successful.

For example, in the case of the lawyer whose children were her motivation, wanting them to have as little upheaval in their lives as possible and ensuring she gave them the best opportunities was the positive angle encouraging her to succeed. The real driver for her, though, was what might happen to them if she *didn't* succeed. They might lose their home, have to change schools, give up their academic tuition and music lessons, move out of the area and she would never be able to offer them the opportunities she and her husband had planned for. The only option in her mind was to create income, finish her studies and become a successful lawyer and property investor.

Most people who have jobs are fairly happy with their lives. They probably don't have everything they want, but they're comfortable, know they could be worse off and, as a result, take the view that they should be grateful for what they have and accept their 'lot'. That's not how entrepreneurs and very successful businesspeople think. They're not necessarily *un*happy, but they know there's more to achieve, have a plan for reaching their goals, and I would guess that all of them have thought hard about the consequences of that not happening and identified some 'pain' drivers.

If you haven't already done it, write down what it would mean to you to be wealthy – where you'd live, what life would be like for you and your family, what car or boat you'd have, how you'd be able to help others more, what you'd be able to do for your friends, where you'd holiday, how you'd spend your time, etc. Now write down the negative consequences of not changing your beliefs and behaviour around money. Look at where you are now and imagine where you might be if things carry on in the same way for the next 20 years. Your list may include getting into debt, using up all your current capital, leaving nothing for your family, working every day for somebody else until you're

65, always wondering 'what if?'... For some people that can be a very sobering experience, and while you shouldn't dwell too much on those painful things – remember, you get what you focus on most of the time! – thinking back to that list every now and then should certainly help keep you motivated.

Modeling and Mentoring

I've touched before on the strength of your network being a key contributing factor to the amount of wealth you'll create and can't stress enough how important it is that you surround yourself with successful people. A good metaphor is a cold tap dripping into a warm basin – the cold droplet is absorbed and the temperature of it raised by the warmth of the larger quantity of warm water. Similarly, a hot drip going into a cold basin will be cooled quickly. If you want to become more like other very successful people, you need to have as warm a basin as possible – i.e. a network which is more successful and wealthier than you and which will constantly raise your success temperature!

In terms of your personal and professional development you need to find people who have achieved the type of success you desire for yourself. Talk to them, ask them questions about significant points in their life and how they approached and handled certain situations; what businesses they are in; what works, what doesn't. It's only by understanding exactly how something was achieved that you can hope to replicate that success.

These people may be businesspeople and entrepreneurs you already know personally, or they may be people you simply know by reputation and admire. Don't be afraid to approach anyone to ask for guidance; you should believe that most people in the world want to help and want to give, and it will probably surprise you what you can get if you just ask. You'll find that most successful people, when told something is impossible, or they can't do it, is not to accept it, but to challenge it, and that's how you need to start thinking if you want to make the most out of every opportunity.

You might not always be able to afford to pay for courses, coaching, access to world-famous entrepreneurs etc. but think about what you have to offer in return. Bartering is the oldest form of interaction, so go into every contact situation with a creative, win-win attitude, and although you will certainly need to invest money somewhere along the line to accelerate your success, you can get some invaluable experience, skills and insight into the patterns that lead to long-term wealth for simply an investment of your time and an exchange of knowledge. It all takes effort, but the time investment you make in your own development will pay dividends in the long-term.

"If you will do what most people won't do
for the next few years,
then you can do what most people
can't do for the rest of your life."
– Carlos Aponte Jr.

Business and Personal Development Coaches

Everything I've talked about so far in this chapter requires motivation, and that's not always easy to achieve. You'll probably feel buoyed up with ideas and good intentions, and promise yourself you're going to go away and take positive steps. However, it's completely natural to find those harder to carry out as time goes on, because you're used to using your time in a particular way and prioritising certain tasks over others, and habits are hard to break. This is where so many people fall down, and unless you make a concerted effort to change and improve how you approach your goals and the challenges and obstacles in your life, you'll never be as successful as you could be.

By far one of the best ways to make sure you follow through with your good intentions is to make yourself accountable to someone, and there's nothing I've found more effective than working with a coach or mentor. Coaches help you establish which areas of your life are out of balance and what obstacles are blocking your path to success, and work with you to move forward in your life and business much more effectively. They challenge your thinking and make you answerable to them, which is a great motivator for achieving the goals you set together. And because a coach is generally someone from outside your business and social circle, they can be completely objective about what changes you need to make.

As with choosing a mentor, you need to find a coach who you like and trust, so you might have to try a few before you find one whose approach really resonates with you. Coaches don't need to be experts in your field of business

– they are working on core skills around time management, problem-solving and overcoming issues and beliefs that are holding you back – but it can help sometimes if they have an understanding or some relevant experience.

If you invest in a business coach, I would recommend you look at getting back double your investment, i.e. if you were to pay out £250 a month for a coach, then you should feel the benefit in increasing your profitability and/or using your time more effectively to the value of £500 a month. For me, personally, investing in my ongoing personal and professional development and associating with successful people has given me the best return of all my investments – better than any property deal I've ever done or any business I've created.

If you would like to be supported by one of the UK's leading wealth coaches, log on to www.platinumpropertypartners. net/freeresources and if you contact us via the website, we will arrange for you to have an initial phone coaching session completely free of charge.

> **"The most expensive thing you will ever own is a closed mind."**

I cannot stress how important this is: don't make the mistake of not investing in your personal and professional development. If you follow that advice, the fruits of this investment will be with you for the rest of your life and you'll be setting a great example to your own children and/ or other family members. If, for whatever reason, you don't invest in a coach or mentor, it's up to you to make sure you really work on motivating yourself so that you don't fall into mistake #7: analysis paralysis.

Personal and Professional Development – Summary

- Log on to www.platinumpropertypartners.net/ freeresources and download the money profiler to identify your potential areas of weakness, then find someone who can either help you change yourself, or find a business partner who complements you, i.e. if you're a spender, try to partner with a saver.
- Get a wealth coach. Contact us via the website address above and we will arrange for you to have a free coaching session over the phone with one of the UK's leading wealth coaching experts.
- 'Out of sight, out of mind': make visual representations of the things you want to achieve – words or images – and keep them pinned up somewhere you'll keep seeing them.
- If someone says, "You can't do that", immediately react like successful and wealthy people do and think, "*How* can I do this...?"
- Remember: your network = your net worth.
- Surround yourself with successful people who are excellent at managing money and take the time to find out how they became excellent.
- If you want to accelerate your development, work with a good coach.
- Commit to spending 20-30 minutes a day learning about investing and investments.

Chapter 9

Mistake #7 - Having a Bad Case of 'Analysis Paralysis'

People suffer from analysis paralysis in all walks of life, but you don't always see signs to identify them. When you're talking about property investment, though, they're much easier to spot. This is especially true at networking events - they're the people listening intently to every free seminar they can find, scribbling pages upon pages of notes, and accumulating a huge stash of literature in a carrier bag. This is the 'shelf help' brigade I referred to earlier in the book! They're fairly knowledgeable, love talking about property, have usually paid quite a bit of money for DVD sets and weekend courses, and will ask lots of questions. But, in almost every case, when you ask whether they've got any investments, the answer will be no. Usually, they're "about to", and "just trying to decide on the right opportunity".

If that sounds like you, try to smile at yourself and read on. You're not alone – we've all suffered from it at some point and the main reason why people have this mental block preventing them from taking action is fear of failure. Analysis paralysis is procrastination, putting off taking the leap, because of fear of choosing the wrong investment route and/or fear of losing money, and it goes back primarily to your attitude towards risk. Someone who's very risk-averse is likely to have a serious case of analysis paralysis, whereas someone who's more optimistic and action-orientated probably won't.

If you are naturally cautious, then don't try to push yourself too far out of your comfort zone because you've seen the pound signs and think you should go for the opportunity that offers the biggest rewards – chances are it's the highest risk. Pick something that's a little more secure, even if it offers lower returns. You don't want to spend the next few years constantly worrying about whether you're going to lose all your savings. Using property to make money is about improving your quality of life, it shouldn't be a headache.

Property is essentially a medium-risk business and often involves investing large sums of money. There are big decisions to be made. If you've had the potential dangers highlighted, been told to spend time doing due diligence, checking out companies and opportunities, and really thinking about why you want to invest and what you want out of that investment, a hesitance to pick just one basket to put your eggs in is entirely understandable. That's particularly true if you don't have a huge amount of capital and are counting on this one investment to give you a certain level of return. So I'm not advising you to rush into making a decision, but you do need to take some action and move yourself forward.

The first questions to ask yourself

How long have you been thinking about property investment - when did you first start seriously looking at the options available to you? If the answer is more than a year and you still haven't actually invested, it's time to address why that is, and the first step is a reality check:

Do you wish you'd started investing 5 or even 10 years ago?

I certainly wish I'd got into property in a much bigger way back in the mid-90s, because if I had, I know I'd have been able to ride the storm that hit me as a result of 9/11 and wouldn't have had to liquidate my business and sell my home. Hindsight is a great thing, and we can all wish we'd done things differently, but none of us has a time machine to go back, nor does time wait for us. Get over your regrets and appreciate that the future is uncertain. If you're having trouble deciding which investment opportunity to go for, chances are you're also agonising over *when* is going to be the best time to invest. Well let me take that pressure off for you, because it's simple and I'll say it again:

The only bad time to buy property is 'later'!

Another way of saying this is 'The best time to buy property is 10 or 20 years ago, but that's not possible, so the second best time is now!'

Of course there are periods when the market's going up and when it's going down, but you can win in both markets, benefiting from good capital growth in boom periods and being able to negotiate hard and get great discounts when it's 'busting'. But if you wait until it's publicly announced that prices are going up rapidly, you'll have missed out on the initial growth spurt, and wasted a lot of time when you could have been getting income from a cash-positive buy to let investment. So forget worrying about the 'when' and concentrate on the 'why' and the 'what'.

There are lots of good investments out there, and now and then you'll come across a great one. If you're too focused on finding the absolute best, the truth is you probably never will. Over-analysis, driven by the fear of making a mistake, is what's preventing you from progressing, so take a step back and reassess what's actually motivating you to make this investment and what you need from it in terms of financial return. That should enable you to discount certain types of opportunities and leave you with something like a shortlist.

Who do you want to work with?

Have you found a company you're happy to work with? Again, if you've been doing the rounds for a year or more, chances are you've identified a few possibilities, but rather than making endless comparisons, go through the due diligence process on two or three and if you're satisfied that they operate with integrity, have a good track record and you find yourself liking the people involved, that should be sufficient for you to at least get started with some confidence.

If you've gone through all those questions and are still unsure about making the leap, it's time to look at the alternatives…

THE 7 BIGGEST MISTAKES MADE BY PROPERTY INVESTORS...

Pain versus pleasure (again!)

If you look at the decision-making process and break it down, you'll find it ultimately comes down to pain and pleasure, as discussed in Chapter 8. People will make a decision and take action more often and more quickly when they're driven by pain, i.e. there is something they're really not happy with and they need to change their situation. If you've been made redundant, for example, then you're far more likely to be looking for a new job, responding to interviews, and maybe considering starting your own business.

So if pain causes a change in behaviour and pleasure tends to sustain it, it follows that if you're relatively happy with your life and there's no real catalyst for change, you're less likely to take a leap into a new field. That could be at the root of your lack of commitment to moving forward. You need to really think about what will happen if you don't make the step to invest. If things are okay for you now, think 5 to 20 years into the future and examine the longer term consequences of not changing, e.g. is your current pension provision going to be enough and what future commitments might you have.

What other wealth creation options are available to you?

We all have an idea of where we want to be, financially, five or ten years from now, but for most people it's a bit of an idle dream. If you're reading this book, presumably you are serious about improving your financial situation, so ask yourself what alternatives to property investment are likely to provide you with the kind of rewards you're looking for. In my opinion and experience, there's nothing that can rival property as a secure money-making vehicle, offering anywhere near the same level of security, capital growth and income generating potential.

If your original motivation for getting into property investment was that you weren't where you hoped you'd be by now, and even after everything you've read, you're still unsure about making your move, make a copy of this next statement and stick it somewhere you can't miss it:

DEFINITION OF INSANITY:
To keep on doing the same things over and over again, and expecting to get a different result.

The path you've taken up until now hasn't provided you with the financial security or freedom you've been looking for, so it's time to take some positive steps and make your move in property!

Getting over 'Analysis Paralysis'

- Accept that what you've been doing up until now hasn't brought you financial freedom, and understand that you need to take the next step now.
- Clarify your motivation: think today about what you want and why.
- Think about your pain versus pleasure: what direction will your life take if you don't take action?
- Find people you're happy to work with – companies and individuals whose success you want to emulate, and who you like and trust.
- Don't get overly focused on finding the absolute 'best' deal – it's enough that you find a 'good' one to get started.

Chapter 10

Next Steps: Shaping your Business Investments for Making your Move

Property is an exciting and rewarding business. It can also be a lot of hard work if you do it all yourself. As a passive investor, there is little or no work to do beyond finding the right partners and investments, but if you choose to be an active investor and build your investment portfolio in a hands-on way, you need to have a wide skill base and be able to multi-task. In Chapter 2, I talked about goals, and if you haven't already started to think about them, here's a recap and some more points for you to consider:

Goals

Ideally, you should be deciding on goals for the next 1, 5 and 10 years so you can plan the short, medium and long-term. Human beings are goal-oriented creatures and everybody has goals - whether you write them down or not, every time you do something, you're working towards an objective. When it comes to property investing, you might not necessarily be able to say what property goals you want to achieve in certain time frames, because, again, you don't know what you don't know, so start with your lifestyle goals.

Probably the easiest to specify are those for the next 12 months, but they'll depend on what you ultimately want to achieve long-term, so picture your ideal future. Whether you do a vision board - putting images on a piece of paper as a visual representation of your goals - a list or a spreadsheet, choose a format that works for you and decide what you want to create in your life. Do you want to work 48 weeks a year and have 4 weeks holiday, or do you want to take 3 months holiday? Would you like to work 3 weeks and then take a week off, or would you like to work 6 months on and 6 months off? What places do you want to travel to, what contribution do you want to be able to make to the world, what material possessions do you aspire to have, what do you want for your family and friends...? Once you have that ideal future, you can start to break it down and don't be afraid to think big. It's a fact that we tend to over-estimate our short-term goals and under-estimate our long-term goals, so make those 5 and 10-year plans really something to get excited about!

The pattern you want and the way you choose to balance work and home life will affect what direction you pursue in your property business, because time off is reliant on passive income. Whether that's achieved by employing staff to take care of the daily running of your portfolio when you're not there, or whether you simply choose to invest in purely passive opportunities is up to you. It will also be dependent on the amount of initial capital you have and whether your primary focus is on having monthly income or lump-sum capital returns. But start with what you *want*, not with what you currently *have*: don't limit your goals by focusing on what you believe is achievable based on your situation today.

One of our Franchise Partners has monthly, 3 monthly, 1 year and 5 year goals - primarily focused on his financial position, portfolio size and structure and time management - which he updates monthly. Another has monthly, 1 year, 3 year and 5 year goals. Here are some highlights from their recent updates:

Primary Aim
- *To become financially free*
- *To have a minimum of £60k passive income per annum*

1 Month Goals
- *I will secure a property with a lease option*
- *I will buy another property 25% or more below market value and recycle all cash invested in 6 months*
- *I will exercise 3 times a week*
- *To secure my new home at a 20% or greater discount*

3 Month Goals
- *I will buy 2 more HMO properties*
- *I will buy one BMV property per month*
- *I will find more sources of finance*

12 Month Goals
- *I will have a passive income of £100k p/a annualised from property*
- *I will have 6-10 PPP HMO properties to generate the income above*
- *I will spend a minimum of 1 hour per day and 4 hours a day at weekends with my children*
- *I will only work 3 evenings per week after 7pm and spend time with my wife & children on the other evenings*
- *I will have a minimum of 4 one week holidays abroad with my family*

- *I will be securing at least one property every 2 months on either a lease option, deferred consideration or BMV basis*
- *I will take tennis coaching once a week*

3 Year Objectives
- *I will have a portfolio generating a minimum of £125k passive income*
- *I will have written a book*
- *I will be have bought a property for my father*

5 Year Objectives
- *I will have £5m of property assets with £2.5m of equity*
- *I will generate a passive income of £150k p/a*
- *I will be able to choose when I work and what kind of work I take on.*
- *I will have a massage or reflexology once a week and visit a health spa 4 times a year*
- *I will have a 2nd home in France*
- *I will own my own sailing boat and use it regularly*
- *I will get my golf handicap to 10 or less*

For the majority of people, one of the primary goals I would encourage is getting to the point where your monthly passive income exceeds your expenses. The day that happens – which I call 'financial freedom day' – it's a huge weight off your mind, knowing you don't have to get up every morning and go out to work to pay the bills. Attaining that first level of financial freedom and replacing your salary-based income through property income should be an 18-36 month plan, and if you want some inspiration, go back and take another look at Neil's story on page 100.

And remember to make your goals visual. Vision boards are great for focusing on the bigger picture, but where you have specific, measurable goals and targets, a simple line graph will show whether you're on target for achieving what you want, in the timeframe you want it. Mark your x and y axis values out, then draw a line from the origin to the top right hand corner, the goal end value. For example, if your passive income was £2,000 a month and you set yourself a goal of increasing it to £4,000 a month within a year, your line graph might look like this:

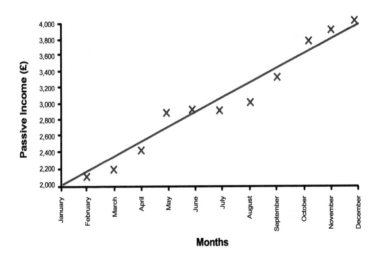

Each month when you mark on the amount of your passive income, it should be as close to the line as possible - if it's above it, you're likely to exceed your goal. Put the graph up somewhere you'll keep seeing it, and tell the rest of your family what you're doing; the more people who know you've set yourself goals, the more likely you are to achieve them.

As your business grows, your goals will change – what you set down today for the next 5 years is not set in stone – because the more you achieve the more you will start to believe is possible.

Preparation is one of the keys to success in any business, and that includes preparing yourself mentally and practically for the 'back of house' activity that's going to keep the engines running. If you're planning to build a portfolio, rather than just make a one-off investment then you shouldn't underestimate how much time you'll need to dedicate to administering your business, particularly when you get involved with refurbishment and renting properties out. You need to be able to hit the ground running. That means being computer literate and familiar with certain basic business practices and terminology, all of which will help you achieve and measure success. If you do have gaps in your skills then find others who can support you.

But how *do* you measure success? Setting weekly, monthly and yearly goals is one thing, but you have to be able to put your achievements and business growth into context in order to make sure your portfolio is on track: you need KPIs.

Key Performance Indicators

KPIs are the metrics by which you analyse opportunities and deals and measure success. Just like having goals, every individual should know what their KPIs are for both their business and their personal life. There are certain KPIs that are common to most businesses and others which will be particular to you, and you set your own KPIs according to what you're trying to achieve.

Any sound business will produce monthly management accounts. These will include:

1. Profit and loss
2. Balance sheet
3. Cashflow and/or P&L forecast
4. Budgets v actuals report

The first two reports are historical while the second two also look into the future, based on your assumptions and what you expect to happen. Without these tools in place you are essentially running your business with a blindfold on. Like it or not, business is a game played primarily by the numbers. If you don't understand your numbers, you don't really have a proper business. Whilst you can delegate some of the financial work that needs to be done, you have to understand your figures and have the right kind of people supporting you. Too many people rely on bookkeepers and accountants, without appreciating that they can only be as good as what you ask them to do for your business.

Don't expect an accountant to make the right decisions for you: they will just act on the instructions that you give them. I learnt this lesson the hard way in 1997 when we employed a full-time bookkeeper in our construction business. Rather than ensuring that she understood the key aspects of how the business operated and the particular complexities of tax, national insurance and other matters, we just let her get on with things. Our accountant did little·

more than file annual accounts and answer the odd query as it came up. Neither were proactive and because we didn't know what questions to ask, we never got the answers we needed. After 18 months we were hit with an unexpected and large corporation tax bill. Shortly after this, we also had to pay £19,000 of tax and National Insurance for 'sub-contractors' who had not paid their own tax and NI. From that point on I set about learning all about the financial management of businesses. It took time and effort but it has rewarded me many times over. You must do the same if you want to be successful.

In addition to financial KPIs, you can measure almost anything you like. In their simplest form, all businesses have three main functions:

1. Sales and marketing: The activities involved in selling and promoting an organisation's goods and/or services.
2. Operations: Ongoing recurring activities involved in the running of a business for the purpose of producing value for the stakeholders.
3. Finance: Matters related to money within the business.

Here is a small selection of some non-financial KPIs that I measure in my property business:

- Number of new tenant enquiries (weekly)
- Number of tenant viewings (weekly)
- Number of rented rooms (weekly)
- Amount of late rental payments (weekly)
- Amount of late rental payments against deposits held (weekly)

- Number of rooms becoming vacant in the next month (weekly)

There are numerous benefits in correctly tracking KPIs like those above. For example, I know that on average, 10 incoming enquiries will lead to three viewings, which in turn will lead to one rented room. Therefore, if my property business has three empty rooms coming up in the next month, the team know that they need to generate at least 30 enquiries to ensure they are filled quickly.

Every Monday morning I receive the above KPI reports in my inbox. I can look at these and very quickly analyse the sales and marketing performance of the business. These are the 'leading indicators' for your rental portfolio and they assist you in ensuring that your occupancy levels stay as high as possible. If you only rely on historical financial management accounts, it is equivalent to running your business by looking in the rear-view mirror. To be effective you need to have a range of KPIs that suit your particular business and situation. As the old saying goes:

> *"If you can't measure it,*
> *you can't manage it."*
> **- Robert Kaplan**

I strongly advise you to determine what business KPIs you want to measure and then implement a system for doing this consistently.

An example of a less common KPI my business partners and I have relates to the amount of time we have to invest in the business on a weekly and monthly basis as a percentage of our overall time. Our goal is that this KPI percentage figure should constantly be reducing over time, while our profitability and income KPI figures are rising so we know we're on track for growing the business while making it more of a passive income stream. That's something you should be striving for - getting maximum results for a reducing amount of time commitment – so knowing what you need to measure and making sure you have a system in place that will accurately record those KPIs should be done as early as possible in the life of your business.

---

holism, *n.* **1.***Philosophy.*
The idea that the whole is greater than the sum of its parts.

If you just have financial KPIs and they're not related to time, quality of life and health, then you can end up getting great financial profit, cashflow and equity growth, but that's no good if you've got to work 7 days a week, 52 weeks a year and your health is declining in the process. You should take a holistic approach to your business and understand what your personal KPIs are, because your motivation for creating and growing your property business should be that you have a better quality of life and standard of living, and that you're able to share that wealth.

As an aside, the French Government recently proposed that countries should not just measure GDP and other financial aspects of the economy, but also include the health and happiness of their populations, as a better measure of the success of the country's performance.

If you forget to measure how your division of time and energy is progressing, you can easily lose focus and end up on a path which is out of synch with your ultimate goal, and you won't understand exactly why, where and how it went wrong.

Administration systems and procedures

I said at the start that you need to be able to multi-task, and before you jump into buying properties you need to understand where your administration strengths and capabilities lie, and what to do about your weaknesses. There is a lot of administration involved, from setting up suitable paper filing systems, to recording expenditure and tracking invoices and receipts related to property refurbishment and management, to reconciling bank statements and being able to produce accurate profit and loss statements and balance sheets. If you've never done anything like this, you need to speak to people who have, and make a decision about whether you learn how to do it for yourself or outsource a lot of the work.

If you've never run a business before, start with your personal finances and look at how you keep track of them at the moment. Do you reconcile statements on an Excel spreadsheet, do you use a basic bookkeeping package, or do you just give your bank statements a cursory glance once a month? Do you know your financial position in terms of assets and liabilities and could you produce a balance sheet or P&L for yourself? If not, you need to address that, because you are currently, in effect, the M.D. of 'YOU, Ltd' and if you don't understand how to manage your own finances, you'll struggle with running your own property business and it will cost you.

Many years ago, I created an easy to use Excel spreadsheet that gives me a snapshot of where I am, financially, and I forecast 12 months ahead. I then update it on a monthly basis to compare budget v actual performance. This same template is successfully used by most of our Franchise and Investment Partners. If you don't already have something like that, I'd urge you to create a spreadsheet which contains the following details:

- Your **monthly income** – including any property income
- Your **monthly expenditure** – broken down into loan/ credit card obligations and other living expenses
- Your monthly income minus your monthly expenditure gives you your **monthly and annual cashflow** figures
- Your **assets** – property, business assets, vehicles, investments and savings
- Your **liabilities** – outstanding mortgage balances, total credit card debt and loans
- Your assets minus your liabilities gives you your **personal net worth**

Rather than you having to reinvent the wheel, I'd be happy to give you a free copy of the one I personally created, which is used by our Platinum Partners. Visit www. platinumpartners.net/freeresources to download your free copy.

Needless to say, your personal net worth should be a positive, not a negative figure! In his book 'The Millionaire Next Door', Thomas Stanley suggests your net worth should be roughly equivalent to:

<u>(Your age) x (Your pre-tax annual salary)</u>
10

While it's certainly not an exact science, it's not a bad benchmark. Although your properties might not contribute significantly to that figure if you're highly leveraged, you should be putting a decent proportion of your income into assets, rather than simply spending it on 'disposables'.

I handed my spreadsheet to my private banking manager when I was looking to move some accounts, and he said that in 25 years he had never had a customer give him such a simple, clear and accurate statement of their personal financial situation. If you know how to do the same for your business and your personal life, you'll be one step ahead when you come to deal with lenders and/or passive investors, and remember that your personal and business finances will have some crossover, so the more detail you understand about both, the more effectively you'll be able to run them. I'd highly recommend downloading the spreadsheet from the PPP website and completing it.

To operate your business in-house, you need to have basic bookkeeping skills and be able to work in an organised and systemised way, and it helps a great deal if you are computer literate. If you're naturally quick on the uptake with computer systems and good with figures, it's probably cost-effective for you to handle everything yourself, and just outsource your end of year accounts to an accountant, but if getting up to speed is going to take a lot of your time and investing money in training, I would suggest you employ a bookkeeper early on.

In terms of your 'Power Team', you might already have an accountant, a bookkeeper and a tax advisor, but check whether they've dealt with clients who have property investments and make sure they have some experience in the field. There are certain requirements and issues that are particular to property investment, and if a bookkeeper, for example, has never dealt with a property business, they may well not even be aware they should be recording things in a certain way. Similarly, your tax advisor might be excellent at dealing with personal and corporate tax, but if he hasn't dealt with a lot of property investment-related businesses, he may not be up to date with the most tax-efficient ways to structure your affairs.

An example of a property investment-specific issue is which items in the refurbishment of a property are considered capital improvements, and which are considered profit and loss items and are therefore tax-deductable. If you're undertaking a major project, the correct allocation of expenditure can make a significant difference to the amount of tax you pay. And while you don't need to be an expert in tax yourself, you should take the time to understand the basics for the purposes of your own accurate bookkeeping, and make sure you are working with a really excellent specialist. It's just one area where paying for expertise will save you that amount many times over.

Now do it!

Remember, you can spend your life looking for the perfect deal, but it's enough just to find a good one. Provided you've put in the time and effort with your preparation and due diligence, you should be able to make a very worthwhile investment, and you can work on refining your technique and getting better deals as you go on.

A final checklist:

- You've got a written list of goals and objectives.
- You've looked at the different investment options out there and decided on the one(s) that fit your financial capital and return requirements.
- You've spent time talking to other successful investors and have identified some mentors or organisations/individuals you're confident can help you move forward.
- You've done your due diligence on property companies and/or markets offering opportunities.
- You know the top 7 mistakes that people make, and how you can avoid them!
- Your administration systems and professional services support network are in place.

People who have properties to sell - whether that's agents, developers or vendors themselves - want to do business, they *want* you to buy from them, so picture yourself in the driving seat and negotiate with confidence. As I've already said, people do business with people they like and trust, and the more you deal with agents, vendors and tenants, the more you'll realise just how true that is, and just how much integrity matters.

And remember, as you go through your property investment journey, to always surround yourself with the best people who will keep raising you up. There will be times when it gets hard, when all your capital seems to be tied up, not every deal will go to plan, and you'll undoubtedly experience 'the dip', but don't be tempted to give up. Follow what successful people are doing, be the person you want to be and never stop learning.

In closing this book I would like to wish you the very best of success in your pursuit to BE more, DO more, HAVE more and GIVE more. I will leave you with these final quotes:

"If a person will advance confidently in the direction of their dream and endeavour to live the life they have imagined, they will meet with success unexpected in common hours."
– Henry David Thoreau

"Life is a daring adventure or it is nothing at all."
– Helen Keller

"When I was young and free and my imagination had no limits, I dreamed of changing the world. As I grew older and wiser, I realised the world would not change. And I decided to shorten my sights somewhat and change only my country. But it too seemed immovable. As I entered my twilight years, in one last desperate attempt, I sought to change only my family, those closest to me; but alas they would have none of it. And now here I lie in my death bed and realise, perhaps for the first time, that if only I had changed myself first, then by example I may have influenced my family and with their encouragement and support I may have bettered my country, and who knows, I may have changed the world."

- Anglican Bishop.
Written around 1100 AD. Taken with permission from the Crypts of Westminster Abbey

Additional Free Resources

We hope you've enjoyed reading this book. If you haven't already, we recommend your next step should be to go to the Free Resources page on our PPP website - www.platinumpropertypartners.net/freeresources - where we've made available all of the following, and more:

- **Financial beliefs questionnaire**: Identify your financial blocks and limiting beliefs so you can work to overcome them
- **Goal setting questionnaire**: This will help you set realistic goals and take a big step towards accelerating your success
- **Assets & liabilities spreadsheet**: get a complete picture of your own financial situation and understand your personal net worth
- **Free wealth coaching session**: a personal coaching session over the phone with one of the UK's leading wealth coaches
- Create your own **Vision board**
- **PPP's top 50 booklist** that will change your life forever
- **The PPP 2009/10 Professional Property Investment Guide**

Downloading and utilising these valuable resources will undoubtedly have a hugely positive impact on your future wealth and success, and if you're ready to find out more, make sure you follow the links online and register to see if you qualify for a free place at one of our upcoming, exclusive

Platinum Discovery Days. Learn about PPP's Franchise and Investment Partnerships, the best ways to maximise cashflow and return on your capital in the current market, listen to Franchise Partners giving real-life case studies and speak to some of the UK's leading financial and property industry professionals about your own personal situation.

www.platinumpropertypartners.net/freeresources

PEACE
ONE DAY

In 1999, filmmaker Jeremy Gilley dreamed that one day all the countries of the world would unite in recognising one day in the year as a day of ceasefire and non-violence. In 2001, the 21st September was officially ratified by the U.N. as International Peace Day and adopted by its 192 member states.

In the days leading up to Peace Day 2009, for the 3rd year in a row, over 1 million children in Afghanistan were vaccinated against polio, in areas that are usually inaccessible to humanitarian workers. All offensive military operations in Afghanistan were halted on Peace Day itself.

Jeremy's latest film, 'The Day After Peace' has been screened in over 90 countries, and the 2008 Peace One Day concert, held at the Albert Hall, has been seen by an estimated 250 million people. The next major objective is to introduce 3 billion people to Peace Day by 2012.

You can help Jeremy achieve his goal simply by making everyone you know aware that the day exists and marking it every year, in even such a small way as lighting a candle.

www.peaceoneday.org

All the profits from this book will be donated to Peace One Day.